UNIVERSAL MEDITATIONS

Recipes for a Peaceful Mind

DAVID LESS

Edited by
Judith M. Allen, Carol Gaskin and Casey Bledsoe

hooh
press

2364 Arden Dr
Sarasota, FL 34232-3861
www.hoohpress.com

Printed in the United States of America
This edition is printed on acid-free paper that meets the American
National Standards Institute Z39.48 Standard
Distributed in the United States, Canada and Europe
by hooh press publications.

Library of Congress Cataloguing-in-Publication Data Less, David.
Universal Meditations, recipes for a peaceful mind / David Less

Cover Design and Logo by Brian Finke
Cover Drawing by Nathan Briggs
Page Design and Production by Marla Camp: Impact Productions
African Healer photo on p. 110 is Aziz Qwabena Offusu-Atta from Ghana

Printed in the US on Recycled Paper.

ISBN: 978-0-578-03727-1

hooh
press

You can find audio demonstrations of meditations in this book, as well as
additional resources, at www.UniversalMeditations.com

Universal Meditations

Recipes for a Peaceful Mind

ACKNOWLEDGMENTS

I have benefited from the experiences and insights of teachers of meditation all over the world. The fact that I was not bound by any particular path has opened numerous doors, and I am grateful to those people who have shared with me the particular nuances and fragrances that have made these meditations profound.

I'm also deeply indebted to those who have taken the time to read the drafts, try the meditations, and offer their wise counsel. Among them are:

Casey Blood, Henry Cretella, Jacob Ellenberg, Kathleen Fitzpatrick, Timothy Fitzwilliam, Emily Kirsch, Priscilla Long, Charlotte Mason, Howard Nelson, Tchukon Shanks and Deborah Angehrn.

Special thanks to Robb Wieselman for his assistance in bringing this book to completion.

I have spent much of my life traveling the world in order to both learn and teach meditation. I wish to thank my wife Anna and my children Una, Vina, Sirr, and Vadan for all the time they spent without me while I was on this quest.

Deep love to my parents, Rose and Jack Less.

Universal Meditations

Recipes for a Peaceful Mind

CONTENTS

Universal Meditations

Recipes for a Peaceful Mind

INTRODUCTION

One rainy afternoon nine years ago in Sarasota, Florida, I was wandering the aisles of one of the mega-bookstores. While browsing through the sections on religion, spirituality, psychology and mental health, as I usually do, I discovered, to my surprise, a whole new section on meditation that had not been there the last time I was in the store. I had already been teaching meditation for over 30 years, and during that time I was happy if I found one new book a year on meditation. Now I saw before me an abundance of volumes large and small.

I pulled a book off the shelf and began to leaf through it. It was filled with teachings about the history, philosophy and value of meditation, the kind of discussion that would engage an academic, but not particularly useful, I thought, for someone wishing to learn to meditate. I began to pull out other titles, and eventually sat down on the oor and spent the afternoon going through books. The common thread seemed to be a lot of words about meditation, and either no instruction at all in how to actually do it, or instruction that was so complex that you would have to be reading it instead of sitting in meditation. The overall impression, it seemed to me, was to make meditation seem far out of reach, available only to a select few.

MEDITATION: HARD OR EASY

Many people are talking and writing about meditation today, so you probably already know that meditation is supposed to be relaxing—that it can help you focus your attention and feel more energy. But you may also have the impression that meditation is impossibly difficult, that it sounds too painful to try to still the mind when you could be dancing, listening to music, watching television, talking with friends, or eating—all activities that seem so much more interesting and inviting.

If you don't understand how meditation works or what it feels like, or if you think that everyone but you knows how to do it, the result is a confused state. Because meditation still seems to have the scent of mystery, or spirituality, or a foreign religion, or prayer, or even of deprivation and denial, people assume that it's not for them, or that it's just too challenging to learn.

In this book, I hope to take the actual experience of meditation and bring it out of its exotic orbit into the realm of everyday life as it is lived by each of us, no matter where or how we live, no matter who we are. What I offer here is a series of meditations that anyone can do, so that you, the reader, can have the actual experience of meditation as it takes place inside your mind and inside your body. These meditations, if followed, will help you learn to meditate, and learning meditation will bring to your life something that is often missing in our technological society: **conscious repose of the mind.**

MEDITATION 101

Let us begin by understanding a few things about what meditation is and what it does.

Meditation is the practice of emptying the thinking element of the mind. Most people equate the thinking element with the whole mind, but it is only one part of the mind. When we quiet this aspect of the mind, we create a space for a higher consciousness to come through. In clear and direct ways, this book offers guidance, instruction and inspiration for those who wish to learn meditation and for practitioners of meditation who are ready to deepen their practice. With this book you will be meditating with ease from the start.

Over the past twenty years, scientific research has shown that meditation produces a relaxed state of mind. This research has revealed that when the mind is in a relaxed state, high blood pressure lowers, sleep difficulties resolve, anxiety diminishes, energy increases, and creativity is enhanced. The proven health benefits of a relaxed mind are numerous, and there is abundant evidence that the practice of meditation produces an overall increase in the power and magnetism of our mental and emotional condition.

THE NEED FOR A MIND IN REPOSE

The world we live in is continually pulling our minds and our psyches outward into intense mental activity. The pressures and stresses of daily life can strain and twist our sense of inner well-being so that it is difficult to find true relaxation unless we go on vacation, and sometimes even then we don't find it. Over time, this lack of ease in our lives strains our relationships, distorts our needs, and dulls our vitality and our creative energy. It can drive us into behaviors and decisions we sense are wrong but don't know how to correct. Not only have we lost our natural rhythm, we can't even remember that we had one.

The constant, even relentless, activity of the mind is a re ec-tion of this strained state. With our many daily responsibilities and obligations at work and at home, we rush out and keep a fast pace, as we multi-task our to-do lists and talk on our cell phones. The rhythm of one thought followed immediately by another and then another is what many people accept and believe to be the normal state of the mind. It may have become so much a part of your life that you do not believe that your mind can ever experience stillness and quiet.

THE MIND IS A MUSCLE

The truth is that any person can meditate. It is not mysterious. The brain is like a muscle, and the mind is like a muscle. We know that practicing new and challenging tasks, like learning a foreign language, chess, or knitting—tasks through which we progress toward ever more advanced stages—develops the brain and trains the mind in new ways. This kind of activity is often deeply satisfying. In fact, the daily practice of anything is challenging and satisfying because it stretches us beyond what we already do automatically. It is an act of consciousness, and it takes us into new territory. So, just as the daily exercise of the body promotes the strength, exibility and health of the body, the daily practice of meditation develops the strength, exibility and health of the mind.

For most people, the idea that the mind is an instrument that can be trained is a new concept. But the mind is even more trainable than the body. When Tiger Woods first burst into the golf world with such great success, there were many interviews with him and his father about the kind of mental training he received which helped him maintain the intense focus and concentration necessary to win tournaments. Both men spoke of the long years of training the mind, in addition to the time devoted to training the golf swing. The strength of the most successful athletes depends on their mental training, because the hard work and perfect form of the body has to occur without mental interference.

STILLNESS

The essence of meditation is not in what you do when you meditate, but rather in what happens behind it. Meditation is the practice of slowing the thinking/feeling/reactive element of the mind in order to create the possibility of stillness. A person may sit in silence for fifteen minutes every day, but if his/her mind is agitated or thick with movement, it is not meditation. Conversely, dancing or playing music, for example, can be meditation when the mind is not thinking and reactive, but rather fully relaxed and suffused with the music or the movement. In this mental stillness, it is possible to experience the reuniting of breath, mind, heart, and body. And as we experience this unity, we begin to feel our natural rhythm come forward.

In creating a space for us to feel our natural rhythm, meditation removes some of the habitual doubts and fears that are the lenses through which we view our everyday lives, so that a more optimistic and positive viewpoint of our being emerges. As our personalities become more comfortable in the conditions of life, we find that meditation helps us discover meaningfulness in situations that otherwise might not seem to have meaning.

Through meditation, we learn to experience a field of consciousness that identifies with oneness—the world and humanity as a whole—rather than with separate or individuated identities. In this way, meditation shows us the inherent value of harmonizing with other human beings, with nature, with the environment, and with ourselves.

Meditation is not exciting. Its goal is stillness, which is the opposite of exciting. But stillness is not passivity. Stillness creates the space to work intentionally with imagination, breath, creativity, memory, feeling, and the senses. Meditation can be playful, imaginative, exploratory. It can also be sensuous. Through the practice of meditation, our senses increase their perception, and our sensual experiences often have a greater depth.

Conscious Intention

Some of the meditations in this book show how to draw on the elements (earth, air, water, and fire) and their distinctive healing properties. Other meditations look to nature, or to the energy of different animals. In each meditation, the mind is active, but it is active according to an inner direction, suggested by the exercise, that can arise as a consequence of stillness. In these meditations, we draw on the natural impulse of the mind to be interested and engaged, and we train this energy toward a calm and harmonious rhythm.

Meditation, like any other skill, must be learned and practiced. You need to have a conscious intention to learn and to practice. You must begin at the beginning — which means you will have to pass through that awkward and uncomfortable stage of being a beginner at something you quite naturally desire to be good at immediately.

Setting Intention

Preparing the Body and Mind

PREPARATION

Getting Ready: Stilling the Body, Becoming Aware of the Breath

The first step toward meditation is learning to still the body. This simple training is at the very core of discipline, concentration, and developing the will. One way to learn this is to insist that the body remain motionless for a certain period of time. It can be as little as two or three minutes, but it conveys the idea to the body and the mind that the mind has the power to control.

Try the following right now. Tell your body it is going to sit still—completely motionless except for the breath—for two minutes, no matter what. Close your eyes, and as you sit, observe how the body will often want to respond by moving, coughing, twitching, scratching, blinking, or some such action that says, "You cannot make me be still."

If we train our bodies to practice being still for two minutes every day (and this can be done with a simple timer), after a while we can sit still for three minutes, then four minutes, and so on. Eventually, the mind can tell the body to be still for half an hour or even longer. As the mind gradually trains the body, the body will eventually respond more naturally and easily to the request for stillness. In time, you can learn to have a quiet mind while the body is in motion. But in the beginning, it is essential to develop the ability to make the body be motionless (but not rigid), and to be able to hold that immovable state for a period of time. As you are teaching the body to be still, you may find that the mind remains active. It is helpful to think of this as a kind of "training period" in which you are meditating even though you haven't yet addressed quieting the mind.

Many people assume that they could never learn to keep the body still for long periods of time, say for one or two hours. However, I know of hundreds of people who live what we would call normal everyday lives who have developed the ability to sit motionless for long periods of time. They have the desire and intention to devote their energy to developing this ability. They set aside a certain period of time each day for the practice of meditation.

FOUR SIMPLE STEPS

There are four simple steps that will help you learn to still the body, and each of these steps will require more energy and attention in the beginning. Then, through repetition, these actions will become automatic.

The first step is to sit on the oor with your legs crossed, if you can. If you can't sit on the oor, sit in a chair, ideally one with a straight back, and put your feet firmly on the oor. If your feet don't reach the oor, place a firm pillow under them. If you can't sit in a chair, but can lie down on your back, this is also an acceptable position. Using a meditation bench is also fine.

If you are sitting on the oor, it is important to raise the pelvis, by sitting on a firm cushion or on folded blankets, as high as necessary for your back to be comfortably straight with your legs crossed. In addition, for most people, especially those past the age of 45, some kind of padding to support the lift of the knees is essential. I use a rolled up cotton blanket, twin-bed size, under each knee. Some people use rolled up or folded towels, or firm pillows. Sometimes when traveling, I use a stack of books with a towel over them. The knees should be resting firmly on the support object and not oating freely in any way. This connects the feeling of the knee to the oor and removes stress on the hip joints.

Take the time to find exactly what you need in order for your body to feel completely at ease. Once you know what you need, you will be able to have everything in one place, and this will simplify the process of setting yourself up each time. Although this may seem complicated, it will make a big difference for your ability to sit longer with greater comfort and stillness. I have students who may spend five minutes or more setting up for only five minutes of sitting in meditation. But the benefit from those five minutes is deep and palpable, whereas sitting for fifteen minutes in even the most minor discomfort will not be beneficial. The body needs to be as comfortable as possible in your chosen position.

Once you are seated, take a deep breath and lift the front of the chest. Then gently move the shoulder blades towards the spine. Align the head over the spine and slightly incline the chin toward the chest. Release all tension from the shoulders. If you have trouble relaxing the shoulders, it is sometimes quite helpful to place a small rolled up hand towel in the armpit under each arm. This helps to keep the shoulder girdle in its proper alignment without any stress on the muscles. Lastly, find a comfortable and natural position for your hands. I rest my hands on my knees, palms down, or I place my hands on my thighs, palms up. Close the eyes gently.

It is also important to keep the jaw relaxed. After one month of practice in sitting, you can touch the tip of the tongue to the roof of the mouth just behind the teeth.

Now we have the body in a comfortable position.

The second step is to send a clear internal message to the body. The message is: "You will maintain stillness for the next period of time (however long you wish to be in meditation)." This may feel artificial or awkward at first, but if you try it, you'll find that its usefulness lies in how it develops the power of the will. The nature of the body is such that as soon as we tell it to be still, it gives us hundreds of reasons why it should move. We must cough, scratch our noses, shift our ankles, lean a little back or forward, or rub our eyes. We have swallowing spasms and a variety of other immediate distractions. But we learn to consciously cultivate the power of the will over the body, and we do this by mentally sending a specific message to the body that lets it know it is no longer in charge.

Initially, you must will the daily practice of meditation into your life. Most people think they have no will power. But will power can be learned. The will develops when you set goals and accomplish them. It develops when you persevere in a certain direction, even though the reasoning mind wishes to stop because of the pain or difficulty of persevering. The will is also developed and strengthened when you sacrifice the immediate pleasure or comfort for the long-term gain. And finally, the will develops by repetition. Actions that promote our well-being, if done repeatedly, always strengthen the will.

Training the body at this point is like training a child, and we must adopt the role of the benevolent parent. Gentle, repeated instruction and encouragement over a period of time gradually changes the habits of the body, so that these habitual "requirements" to move will disappear. We must be simultaneously firm and gentle. I remember silently speaking to my leg that had to stretch, and telling it, "If you just wait ten minutes, you can have the most delicious stretch, so please be a little patient, and I know you'll enjoy the reward."

It is important that the body knows how much time it is expected to be still. Use a timer (a simple kitchen timer will do, or the timer on a watch or digital alarm clock), so the body can train itself to be still for a defined period of time. When you begin meditating, it's better if the room is quiet, and if that's not possible, earplugs sometimes help. In the beginning, it is also helpful to meditate in low light rather than bright light. In addition, the mind needs to know that it will have an uninterrupted period of time devoted to awareness of itself, relaxation, inner awareness, and inner quiet. So turn off phones, put a do-not-disturb sign on the door, and meditate during a period of time when you aren't expecting guests. Lastly, I recommend choosing a particular place in your home and specific time of day for meditation each day, as the body and mind are positively in uenced by establishing rhythm and regularity.

Now we have a comfortable body, and we have a still body.

The third step is awareness of the breath. Of all the instructions given about meditation, the most important one is to remember the connection between one's consciousness and the breath. Breath awareness can transform meditation from an experience of a quiet mind to a life-changing event.

Every time you sit in meditation, the beginning should be the breath awareness. Take a moment to watch your breath, feeling the breath as it comes into your lungs and as it goes out. This is the point at which the timer starts. Unless instructed otherwise by a specific meditation, the breath should be even and normal. The breath should not be deeper or shallower than your breath is when not in meditation (so it is helpful to notice how your breath is in the course of your daily activities).

Be the observer of the movement of your breath. Feel as if the breath is a pendulum that swings inward and outward. Make the breath smooth, without any pauses or hitches. Make the breath feel round, even at its outer edges, as it rises and falls naturally.

Now we have a comfortable, still body with breath awareness.

The fourth step is for those of us who at this point have a sudden rush in our minds about all of the things we must do that need our attention. I suggest that you begin the meditation with a pen and paper next to you, and at this point, list all the needs or stresses, letting yourself know that these will be addressed after the meditation is complete. Here again, we are engaging the will by taking charge of how the next period of time will unfold.

Some people find this step unnecessary, and many do it only as they're learning to meditate. However, I have a friend who is a rabbi in his eighties who experiences ecstatic meditation, and he still uses this technique.

The mind has rhythm, and the rhythm of the mind is slow to change. Many people expect that when they sit down for meditation, they will go immediately into an altered state. The actuality is usually quite different. You may remember the first time you tried to ride a bicycle, ski downhill, or drive a car. It seems as if it should be easy, and for some people, it really is. But for most of us, it's a slow process of learning and practice.

Often when people are learning to meditate, their minds actually speed up during meditation, creating a rhythm that is somewhat uncomfortable. This is just one of many reasons why people end up believing they can't meditate or that it doesn't work for them. It helps in the beginning phase if we understand why the mind does this.

There are two reasons that the mind initially increases its activity when we are learning to meditate. The first is that the mind is not accustomed to experiencing moments without external stimulation. The second reason is that when we meditate, we focus our attention on the mind, and the mind is used to being the instrument that is doing the focusing. In other words, the mind is not accustomed to being looked at; it's used to being that which does the looking. In its discomfort, it creates more mental energy—increases its rhythm—in the effort to use the act of thinking to resolve this new and unfamiliar condition.

Initially, it might seem difficult to expend the necessary effort to train the body. However, all of the effort will be rewarding to both the body and mind when deeper and quieter states of awareness are experienced. The human body is the temple of the universe, but every temple, even the universal ones, must be built from a strong foundation.

How long should you meditate? Meditation of any length is better than no meditation. If you only have five minutes, it is better than none at all. Ideally, twenty minutes in the morning and twenty minutes in the evening is a minimum. But since we don't live in an ideal world, if you can only make space for fifteen minutes in the morning and nothing in the evening, then do that. As you become more proficient in meditation, longer and longer periods of meditation will naturally occur.

Initially, the way to train the body to be still is to start with very short periods of time, three or four minutes. Each week, add a minute or two or more if you have no difficulty in keeping the body still. Build up to twenty minutes.

There is an old story that coffee was discovered by practitioners of meditation who would often fall asleep in the midst of their meditations. This shows us that the problem of sleeping through meditation has been around for a while. Many of the meditations in this book offer the mind enough stimulation to stay awake and enough evenness of mind to experience peace. If you find yourself frequently drifting into sleep during meditation, make sure you are getting enough rest in the night, and do your meditation in the morning, when it is easier to stay awake. Also it must be noted that meditation relaxes the mind of some people who cannot normally relax, so the few minutes of sleep experienced in meditation can be quite beneficial.

When you are sitting comfortably, remember these steps:
  • Gently lift the chest
  • Gently shift the shoulder blades toward the spine, and relax the shoulders
  • Gently draw the chin slightly back, so that you feel the back of the neck lengthen
  • Slightly incline the chin toward the chest

UNIVERSAL MEDITATIONS

RECIPES FOR A PEACEFUL MIND

HOW TO USE THIS BOOK

This book is composed of 72 meditations, divided into 12 weeks, each with its own theme. Those who already have a regular meditation practice might choose to move through the book in their own way, as they seek out the recipes they have a taste for. Just reading the meditations without actually practicing them is like assembling the ingredients for a dish, but not cooking it, and thus not eating it. You can read the book from beginning to end and do the meditations in order, or you can choose the meditation that suits the need of the day. Some days, for example, I will focus on nature in my meditations because I might be in a hotel room in the middle of a city and need to bring the feeling and images of mountains into my consciousness.

These are suggestions, not rules. Some people might read through every meditation and decide to develop their own system and technique for choosing. There is no such thing as meditation police. I have been teaching meditation all over the world for thirty-five years, and these suggestions are only what seem to be most effective for most people.

At the beginning of each meditation, you will find a one- or two-line "Mini-Meditation." Read the sentence and take a minute or two to think about its meaning. This will help take you out of your usual, daily mind mode and direct you

You can find audio demonstrations of meditations in this book, as well as additional resources, at www.UniversalMeditations.com.

towards your deeper self. You may also read the sentence several times out loud.

One purpose of these short meditations is to direct us towards a more relaxed state. They signal to our reactive minds that it is now time to become more re ective. Reading them and re ecting on their content before entering the meditations constitutes a brief ritual that directs us toward the meditative mode. In this way, the Mini-Meditations condition the mind to enter a state of quiet.

In addition, the Mini-Meditations are concentrated enough to convey a subtle message to our consciousness quickly. On those days when there just isn't time for a twenty-minute meditation, these short offerings will keep the practice in a regular daily rhythm.

After the Mini-Meditation, you will find the main meditation of the day. When you begin a meditation, first read through it a few times. Write down the critical steps, or keep the book open in front of you. Read step one, then close your eyes and try it. If at that point you don't remember step two, open your eyes and read step two. Continue this until you've experienced the whole meditation.

Be aware that when you are learning the meditations, they might take longer than the suggested times. The goal is to be very familiar with the meditation, so take whatever time is appropriate.

You can do a new meditation daily as the book suggests. Alternatively, you can practice one meditation for several days before going on to the next. Don't judge the meditations in advance. At the end of four or five days, you'll be able to feel if you have an affinity for that meditation.

It is helpful to keep notes in the book or in a journal about how you experience each meditation, and whether you feel you would like to repeat this meditation on a longer basis.

Sometimes I use terms that you may not be accustomed to hearing. If you do not understand something as clearly as you wish to, just let your imagination create whatever meaning emerges at the moment of doing the meditation. By going ahead and attempting the meditation, you will gain insight into what may have seemed confusing initially. So even if you feel the instructions are not at the level of clarity you desire, try the meditation with an open mind and a bit of confusion, and observe what happens.

Remember that this is not a class where the goal is to be smarter or get a perfect grade. The meditations are a process designed to help you move towards a less reactive state and to live with a greater sense of peace and well-being.

The Commentary section of the Day's Meditation will provide you with some food for thought and suggest possible re ections on the theme. Let them nourish you without too much effort.

A Final Word About Learning

There are natural rhythms in our lives, and these rhythms have an effect during the learning process. There will be times when your ego will have a long list of reasons why meditation is not possible that day or that week. When you don't feel like meditating, your rhythm is moving to direct your consciousness outward rather than inward. It is common when people practice inner concentration, turning inward for three days, for example, that on the fourth day there will be a strong tendency to change the direction of the focus toward the outer world.

When learning, it is wise to train yourself to overcome these tendencies and make a vow that, regardless of circumstances, every day for a specified period of time, you will find some time for meditation. In this way, a deeper rhythm has time to become dominant over the shallower rhythm. This deeper rhythm, when nurtured, creates in us a firmly rooted power of will and diminishes the pull of the reactive mind.

If you decide to make meditation a part of your daily life, as I hope you do, I suggest you wait at least three months before evaluating your progress. Make a commitment to try these meditations on a daily basis for three months. At the end of this period, you will see a subtle, or not so subtle, shift in your energy level and in your relationship with your mind and environment.

It is also desirable to have at least some modicum of faith that practicing meditation will eventually bring quiet to the mind and lighten the psyche. As with many new projects in our lives, the initial enthusiasm diminishes in time, and faith needs to be present to bridge the gap between initial enthusiasm and long-term results. You can always turn to the history of meditation and remember that this practice is thousands of years old, has existed in many different kinds of civilizations, and continues its popularity today. There must be something to it.

MEDITATION: IN REVIEW

Posture

> Find a comfortable sitting position
>
> Gently lift the chest, shift the shoulder blades toward the spine; relax the shoulders
>
> Slightly incline the chin toward the chest
>
> Find a comfortable place for your hands and close your eyes gently
>
> Relax the jaw and tongue

Message to your Body

> Send a clear internal message: "You will maintain stillness for the next period of time."

Awareness of the Breath

> Observe the movement of your breath
>
> Feel the breath as it comes in and goes out
>
> Make the breath smooth and regular like a pendulum

Relaxing the Mind

> Let the mind identify with the breath
>
> Allow yourself to find a balance between a free-owing imagination and a directed mind
>
> Remember that the brain is like a muscle that strengthens with exercise
>
> Trust that you will become proficient

You are the owner of this book and the owner of these meditations. Use them with Joy and Diligence, and Beauty will result.

UNIVERSAL MEDITATIONS

Week One

Meditations in the Heart

INTRODUCTION

In practicing meditation, the heart has a greater role than the head. Many people practice meditation to quiet the mind, but ultimately what quiets the mind is an awakened heart. The heart referred to is not just the physical organ but is rather a certain sensitivity within each of us that can be enhanced through the practice of meditation. Directing memory and emotion in conjunction with our breath is the way to awaken the heart. The following meditations will create sensitivity and awareness in the heart.

MEDITATIONS IN THE HEART

MONDAY

Mini-Meditation

The beauty and harmony of nature is an expression of my own heart.

Meditation

(First part 5 minutes maximum; second part as long as you like)

1. Recall the most heartfelt place you have ever been—a place that moved you deeply or evoked a beautiful feeling you cannot quite put into words. Create the image of that place as you remember it, including sounds, smells, and other sensory and visceral memories. Allow a feeling of that place to emerge and allow your heart to soften; sit with that feeling for a minute or two.

2. If you wish, jot down your impression of this place with a short description, a poem, a sketch. Save what you have created and refer to it several times during the day. Each time, take a minute to be aware of your feelings.

Commentary

In this meditation, we use memory, imagination, creativity, and emotion to change the rhythm of the everyday mind. It is a "pause that refreshes," but instead of a Pepsi, we use the beauty of nature to relax the heart. If you follow the second part, both writing and referring to what you have written or sketched will enhance your awareness of your emotions throughout the day.

MEDITATIONS IN THE HEART

TUESDAY

Mini-Meditation

The beauty of the universe is reflected in the face of the innocent child.

Meditation

(7 to 10 minutes)

1. Recall the most heartful person you've ever met—someone with whom you felt an inexplicable affinity, whose heart spoke to your heart. Imagine that person is sitting with you at this moment, perhaps even holding you (if that is appropriate).

2. Imagine that their beautiful and loving heart is actually your heart. Sit with this experience for five to ten minutes.

Commentary

Here we practice one of the great secrets of meditation: concentration on other than self. Often it is easier for our creativity to function if we allow it to imagine another person. By imagining another's heart to be our heart, we naturally diminish the grip of the ego.

Week One

Meditations in the Heart

WEDNESDAY

Mini-Meditation

The joy of my soul moves my heart to dance.

Meditation

(5 to 15 minutes)

1. Close your eyes and hear/feel the pulse of your heart. If you have difficulty, place your fingertips lightly on your carotid artery, wrist, or other place in the body where you can more easily feel the pulse.
2. With each beat of the heart, silently think the word LOVE. Continue for one to three minutes.
3. Then switch to the word JOY for one to three minutes.
4. Next, think the word BEAUTY for one to three minutes.
5. Be aware of your pulse and your breath simultaneously for one minute.

Commentary

Many meditations start by attuning us to the rhythm of the pulse. It is quite common for the mind to move at a rhythm that is much faster than the pulse. Placing our attention on the heartbeat has the effect of slowing our minds and making us aware that we have an inner, palpable clock that we can train ourselves to glance at from time to time. By aligning a feeling with our heartbeat, we begin to learn that we can create and direct what we experience.

WEEK ONE

MEDITATIONS IN THE HEART

THURSDAY

Mini-Meditation

My heart is a doorway that is always open.

Meditation
(6 to 9 minutes)

1. Visualize a beautiful, open archway in the center of your chest, around the area of the sternum, and allow the current (or feeling) of your breath to ow in and out of that arch. Continue for one to three minutes.
2. When you can feel the current clearly, imagine that you are breathing light and energy in and out. Continue for one to three minutes.
3. If/when you can experience both energy and light, breathe love in and out. Continue for one to three minutes.

Commentary

For many people, meditations that focus on the heart are the easiest to experience. Here we introduce the awareness of the heart center (chakra) and the light and energy in the breath. You can practice this meditation two or three times a day, until you can easily experience a sensation in the center of the chest. Notice the distinction between light and energy. We perceive light; we experience energy.

WEEK ONE

MEDITATIONS IN THE HEART

FRIDAY

Mini-Meditation

Heaven and earth meet in my heart.

Meditation

(7 to 10 minutes)

1. This meditation is for the relaxation of the heart. Feel your pulse, either physically with your hand or by becoming very quiet and sensing it within.
2. Breathe love, light, and energy in and out of the heart center in the middle of the chest.
3. With each breath, imagine the heart center releasing (giving up) any impressions that are covering its pure state. Do not evaluate or judge where these impressions come from or why any particular impression comes to your mind or heart. Continue for five to ten minutes.

Commentary

In this meditation, we introduce the ability to self-purify. The intention to release impressions will do more to release them than evaluating what is good or bad, or what should be kept and what let go. It is important not to get overly involved with the impressions being released, but instead to be simply the observer.

MEDITATIONS IN THE HEART

WEEKEND

Mini-Meditation

If your heart could see,
how would it see you?

Meditation

(12 to 20 minutes; 3 to 5 minutes per section)

1. Place the thought or feeling of forgiveness in your heart; with each exhalation let it spread slowly to every cell in your body. Next, let the sense of forgiveness spread to all thoughts in your mind. Then let it spread to all feelings in your emotional body.

2. Place the thought or feeling of courage in your heart; with each exhalation let it spread slowly to every cell in your body. Then let the sense of courage spread to all thoughts in your mind. Then let it spread to all feelings in your emotional body.

3. Place the thought or feeling of depth in your heart; with each exhalation let it spread slowly to every cell in your body. Then let the sense of depth spread to all thoughts in your mind. Then let it spread to all feelings in your emotional body.

4. Place the thought or feeling of love in your heart; with each exhalation let it spread slowly to every cell in your body. Then let the sense of love spread to all thoughts in your mind. Then let it spread to all feelings in your emotional body.

Commentary

Just as the blood of the whole body is continually passing through the heart, this meditation draws our suggested thoughts and feelings through the heart. It also reminds us that we can affect our consciousness at the cellular level. In other words, we are touching the DNA with a chosen aspect of consciousness. After you have mastered this meditation, it can be continued on a daily basis if you choose.

Week Two

Meditations on Beauty

INTRODUCTION

In practicing meditation, we must appreciate that which we see with our eyes outwardly as well as that which we perceive inwardly. Beauty, which is the manifestation of love, can be appreciated and digested in such a way that it creates in us a desire for wholeness. Beauty is the gift that naturally inspires the heart and the mind to seek for deeper states of being.

For those new to meditation, beauty can be an inspiration and catalyst for changing one's consciousness. If our eyes are open to beauty, we see the miracle of creation in the face of an infant, the colors of a sunset, and the movement of the wind. More importantly, we see the subtle beauty behind the manifested beauty. When we experience beauty this way, meditation changes from an exercise to a blissful gift.

MEDITATIONS ON BEAUTY

MONDAY

Mini-Meditation

The flower of the rose is love manifested.
The thorn of the rose is beauty hidden.

Meditation

*(30 seconds per section: if the meditation is repeated,
build up to 3 minutes per section.)*

1. Look at the picture of the rose.
2. Close your eyes and imagine it in great detail. Then open your eyes again.
3. Close your eyes and see the rose in three dimensions within.
4. Imagine the smell of the rose.
5. Optional: Remember the perfume throughout the day.

Commentary

This is the first meditation requiring the use of a prop. Either use the photo included here, or enjoy finding the picture of the perfect rose for you. Or you may use a real rose. If you use a real rose and you wish to repeat this meditation, then the object of concentration will change each time you repeat the meditation, which makes it more difficult. On the other hand, it is often easier to concentrate on a living object than a picture.

The goal of this meditation is the practice of re-creating and holding an image in your mind. This concentration of mind is one of the basic building blocks for successful meditation.

TUESDAY

Mini-Meditation

A beautiful memory from the past creates beauty in the present.

Meditation
(7 to 15 minutes)

1. List the three most beautiful memories of your life so far—experiences of epiphany involving a person, place, or occurrence. Include at least one memory from childhood and one from young adulthood.
2. Now feel the emotion behind the first memory. Note it on your list.
3. Do the same with the second and third experiences.
4. Find these emotions in you now, and see if they are present in your life. If they are present, enhance them by your thought. If they are not present, invite them in by the use of your imagination.

Commentary

This meditation directs the memory to a positive goal. Memory, which is one aspect of the mind, can be affected by what we choose to remember. By placing beauty before the screen of the mind, the functioning of the mind becomes more harmonious and beautiful. This meditation is strongly recommended for people whose work is very analytical.

WEDNESDAY

Mini-Meditation

When the tree of love produces fruit,
this is beauty.

Meditation

(5 to 10 minutes)

1. Imagine a beautiful tree with roots that spread deep into planet Earth and pull from planet Earth peace and love. The trunk is made of perseverance and loyalty, the leaves from joy, and the fruit from beauty.
2. Imagine each of the four sections for one minute apiece:

> Roots.....Peace and Love
> Trunk.....Perseverance and Loyalty
> Leaves....Joy
> Fruit......Beauty

Commentary

This meditation is very effective for people who can never seem to root themselves in this world. The image of a tree rooted in planet Earth creates a subconscious attunement to stability and solidity. If you have trouble doing this meditation visually, practice by drawing or painting the image of the tree.

Week Two

Meditations on Beauty

THURSDAY

Mini-Meditation

It is the innocent who experience beauty.

Meditation

(5 to 10 minutes)

1. Look at each of the above images for one minute.
2. After looking at each one, close your eyes and be aware of the feeling it has evoked.

Commentary

This simple meditation, done consistently for a few days, can connect you with hidden feelings about the nurturing aspect of your being, about death and aging, and about relationships with the feminine. Gradually this meditation shifts the consciousness from the reactive mentality to a more intuitive, circular modality. There is a deeper level to this meditation whereby one experiences transcendence.

Week Two

Meditations on Beauty

FRIDAY

Mini-Meditation

*Pure sound leads to the
experience of beauty.*

Meditation
(5 minutes)

1. You will need a clear, resonant bell or chime of some kind. A wine glass half-filled with water or a crystal bowl will work well.
2. Sit comfortably and strike the bell or chime four times a minute for five minutes. Attenuate your sense of listening.

Commentary

Notice the moment the sound is created...the echo of the sound...the memory of the sound...and the noise of silence. We can train any of our senses to work backwards from the physical reaction to an outside stimulus, to an inner sense of awareness that is not defined by outside events. In this state, the sense is not merely passive, but actually is creative. For example, we may use our eyes as organs of conductivity as well as receptivity.

Week Two

Meditations on Beauty

WEEKEND

Mini-Meditation

Beauty is the manifestation of love, and love is the creator of beauty.

Meditation
(20 minutes)

1. Imagine five people in your life whom you have loved. List them. See if you can recreate the strong passion for each of those people that you felt at the height of the relationship. Feel that passion in the heart center. Encourage the heart to give birth to a beautiful manifestation of that feeling. It may be a beautiful form, thought, or feeling, or a poem, line of music, or symbol.

2. While keeping the consciousness focused in the heart, breathe in and think, "Beauty is...." Breathe out and think, "...the expression of love." Repeat for a minimum of ten or a maximum of twenty breaths.

Commentary

This meditation is not intended to recreate passion on a personal level. The memory of the passionate love we had for a person is a seed thought that ignites the energy of passion in our heart. We then continue in this meditation to use that energy of passion to create beauty. This meditation trains us to balance passion. If you happen to awaken in the night, the second part is a good practice to remember.

Week Three

Meditations on Nature

INTRODUCTION

Nature is a great holy scripture that can inspire the soul of human beings. It is a wonderful teacher of harmony and cycles—life and death, action and repose, limitation and freedom—and the ever changing yet always repetitive nature of life.

Many indigenous peoples absorb the mysteries of nature and use them in prayer and meditation. Today, in cultures where so many live separate from nature or have an experience of nature that is manufactured or artificial, we have lost this outer connection. By meditating on the symbols and ways of nature, we reconnect with the primal need in human beings to experience that which is vaster, older and more powerful than ourselves.

Thousands of years ago, beautiful places in nature became temples and shrines. Those memories still exist in the subtle minds of each of us and can be rekindled by nature meditations. As you practice these meditations, a feeling of connectedness with the planet will hopefully emerge.

MONDAY

Mini-Meditation

The courage to be our natural self is both the challenge and the gift of life.

Meditation on an Animal
(12 minutes)

1. Choose one of these options:
   Spin your chair around twice;
   Stand up and turn in a circle twice; or
   Take two slow breaths.
   Then be aware of whatever animal comes into your consciousness.

2. Visualize your animal sitting, standing, swimming, or ying in front of you. Ask it to guide you to a place of:
   a. Peace
   b. Protection
   c. Clarity
   d. Inspiration
   or a combination of any or all of the above.

3. Stay in the place of your choice for ten complete breaths and experience the mood of that place.

4. If you wish, at the end of the ten breaths ask the animal for any message from the natural world.

Commentary

Many people believe meditation to be some onerous exercise in serious spirituality. This meditation invokes the child within each of us, allows our minds to play, while at the same time the message we receive can be very profound, life-giving, and supportive. One of the reasons the ancients used animals as totems was to symbolize the strengths, powers, and different aspects of wisdom latent in each human being. Imagining the breath of an animal can draw those latencies to the surface.

If this meditation makes you very self-conscious, close the door.

MEDITATIONS ON NATURE

TUESDAY

Mini-Meditation

We never fully arrive at the purpose of life,
as it is as alive and growing as we are.

Meditation on a River

(15 minutes)

1. See your whole life as a river...your birth a thin stream of water emerging from all the waters of the earth. The river gently trickles during childhood, then encounters a few waterfalls during the teen years.

2. Now you, the meditator, take over from here. Let the river ow where it will. The water might run in little rills or huge torrents—like the mighty Mississippi or the creek through your backyard—muddy or clear, the banks lush with foliage or silted with sand.

3. See your life as a river meeting other rivers owing to the sea.

Commentary

Meditating on the water element produces a sense of healing and also a sense of overcoming. The ow of water is a very soothing image for our psyches, even if it is rushing through a canyon. It is no coincidence that many of our ancient relatives used natural springs and spas as places for healing, purification, and recovering a natural state of balance. Water is also symbolic of the power of patience and gentleness. We know how, in time, a ow of water can create a great chasm. We know that water goes over and around its obstacles rather than through them.

MEDITATIONS ON NATURE

WEDNESDAY

Mini-Meditation

What I desire with my mind is limited by my mind. What I desire with my heart is limited by my depth of heart. What my soul desires is born and lives without limitation.

Meditation on the Four Phases of the Moon
(10 minutes)

1. Visualize a sky with many stars and no moon. Be aware that the moonless, starry sky represents potentiality. Hold the image for at least one minute.
2. Visualize the same sky with the addition of the tiny sliver of the brand new moon. Be aware that the new moon embodies the energy of receptivity. Hold this image for at least one minute.
3. Visualize a sky with fewer stars and a quarter moon. Be aware that the quarter moon represents the energy of inspiration. Hold this image for at least one minute.
4. Visualize a sky with still fewer stars and a three-quarter

moon. Be aware that the three-quarter moon represents attainment. Hold this image for at least one minute.

5. Visualize a sky with no stars and a full moon. Be aware that the full moon represents completion and stillness. Hold this image for at least a full minute.

Commentary

The moon is a wonderful multi-faceted symbol. Its life cycle is short and regular; its changing energy is visible. The knowledge that it is in perpetual relationship with the sun may remind us of our relationship with the Infinite. Train yourself to be aware of the phases of the moon and how they affect your life. Observe the value of starting projects in the new moon cycle, and being more restful when the moon is waning. Another lunar meditation is to lie on the ground and allow one's body, mind, and spirit to be washed by the light of the moon.

THURSDAY

Mini-Meditation

Blessing is the natural state of the soul.

Meditation on the Ocean
(9 to 12 minutes)

1. Visualize a calm and peaceful ocean.
2. Imagine the light breeze blowing, and a gentle roll begins on the surface of the water.
3. The breeze becomes a steady wind, and waves appear.
4. The wind grows strong, and the waves grow in height.
5. Visualize large waves and a strong wind, and feel the power of inspiration and upliftment.
6. Gradually bring the ocean back to a calm and peaceful state, and feel the power of peace.

Commentary

Notice the relationship between water and air, and wave and ocean, in this meditation. Each wave is an expression of the ocean and yet is not the whole ocean. The wind, the weather, and the moon raise the waves; they live for a moment and return to the ocean, only to be reborn a moment later as another wave. Some of the water from the original wave might be in the new wave. The wind might get stronger and so create larger waves on the surface of the ocean. But no matter what the conditions on the surface, underneath it all, just a few feet below the surface, there is peace.

FRIDAY

Mini-Meditation

A moment of rest, love comes naturally forth.

Meditation on Breath and Nature
(12 to 15 minutes; each section 2 to 3 minutes)

1. Breathe in shallow breaths as you think about a rock that you know.
2. Breathe in long breaths thinking about the rock. Now breathe in normal breaths thinking about the rock.
3. Think about a lake or a river or a pond that you know. Breathe in long breaths thinking about the body of water. Now breathe in normal breaths thinking about the body of water.
4. Think about a plant that you know. Breathe in long breaths thinking about the plant. Now breathe in normal breaths thinking about the plant.
5. Think about an animal you know. Breathe in long breaths thinking about the animal. Now breathe in normal breaths thinking about the animal.

6. Think about a person you know. Breathe in long breaths thinking about the person. Now breathe in normal breaths thinking about the person.

Commentary

This is an adaptation of a classical meditation in which we begin to experience the relationship between breath, thought, and the content of the thought. You want to be aware of the experiential difference between your breath as you think of a rock and your breath as you think of a plant. As we grow in our ability to affect our mind with meditation, a natural by-product is the skill to change the content of our mind at any moment. We learn that a long breath fixes certain thoughts in the mind and a shallow breath encourages uidity. We can also learn that it is not necessary to fixate on thoughts that have no real product.

Meditation enhances the experience of everyday life. Meditation is not separate from life. What we learn in meditation is meant to be applied in life.

WEEK THREE

MEDITATIONS ON NATURE

WEEKEND

Mini-Meditation

Trust develops by experiencing the over-whelming power of the storms of nature.

Meditation

(15 minutes minimum)

1. Visualize being in a powerful windstorm. Feel the power of the wind as it blows the thoughts away from your mind.
2. Now, add lightning to the storm. Visualize being struck by lightning, and in that moment feel your mind become filled with light. Allow the lightning to strike again and again, and each time allow the mind to take in more and more light. Find in yourself the power that is expressed in the lightning.
3. Try to identify with the power that is behind the power of the storms.

Commentary

This meditation combines the powerful forces of purification and illumination. Much of our mental energy and process can be associated with the air element, hence the use of air as the windstorm to clear away the thoughts from the screen of the mind. Anyone who has been outside in a strong wind knows that extraneous thought disappears as we focus on just standing up. Use the will to focus on the wind, and the wind will do its part to clear the mind naturally.

There is an ancient story that the Prophet Moses was illuminated when struck by lightning. In this meditation, we allow any imaginings about lightning's potential harm to fall away, so we can just absorb the immense quantity of light contained in lightning. This will help us discover the infinite light that can be experienced in each human being.

MEDITATIONS ON SCIENCE AND SPIRIT

INTRODUCTION

Science is a process of asking questions and finding answers. Each answer leads to a greater question which leads to greater answers. It is also important to understand that science as we know it is based upon what we think we have learned in the past. As we grow, and our questions grow greater, some of this presumed knowledge proves not to withstand the test of time. There are laws and theorems that have been uprooted as human understanding grows. So science becomes the art of interacting with that which is still alive and releasing that which is no longer truth.

In these meditations, we are guided to use those principles that are in accordance with our current belief systems to raise our consciousness. However, the meditator is seeking answers that are far greater than any of the principles used in these meditations. Our natural questioning nature is quieted by the answer that uproots the question. In this way, science becomes living and active in the mind, heart and spirit.

MEDITATIONS ON SCIENCE AND SPIRIT

MONDAY

Mini-Meditation

The sphere is love at rest;
the pyramid love in activity.

Meditation

(1 minute for each image, increasing to 3 minutes. To get the full benefit of this meditation, it should be done for at least three days. Ideally, it can be practiced over a long period of time—months as opposed to days.)

Tools: On one sheet of unlined paper, draw a circle one-half inch in diameter—the size of the end of a AA battery. On a second sheet, draw an equilateral triangle with each side measuring one-half inch.

1. Look at the circle for ten seconds. Close your eyes and visualize the circle. When you can hold the image of the circle, open your eyes.

2. Close your eyes again and visualize the circle in three dimensions, as a sphere. When you see the sphere clearly, open your eyes.

3. Close your eyes again and imagine the sphere filled with color. Hold the concentration for thirty seconds.

4. Look at the triangle for ten seconds. Close your eyes and visualize the triangle. When you can hold the image of the triangle, open your eyes.

5. Close your eyes again and visualize the triangle in three dimensions, as a pyramid. When you see the pyramid clearly, open your eyes.
6. Close your eyes again and imagine the pyramid filled with color. Hold the concentration for thirty seconds.
7. Now in your mind, bring the pyramid inside the sphere.

Commentary

This is the classic introduction to the practice of concentration as taught in many mystical schools. We look at an archetypal image with the physical eyes and recreate it with the inner eye until we can do this with any object. When you develop this skill, your relationship with meditation and with life will change. Until you have concentration, your experience in meditation and in life is as if you are visiting a foreign country without speaking the language; it's enjoyable, but not the complete experience.

The second step of transforming a mental image from a two-dimensional shape to a three-dimensional one is a leap of concentration that will bring you much energy. The third step of adding color to the image heightens the experience even more. Some people love this meditation, while others respond more readily to meditations that emphasize an emotional content.

TUESDAY

Mini-Meditation

Form both hides essence and reveals it.

Meditation
(12 minutes)

1. Think of a physical substance that you handle daily. Some examples are water, a food, wood, rocks and gems, esh, plastic, etc.

2. In your mind, divide the substance into half the quantity you thought of first.

3. Keep dividing the substance into smaller and smaller portions until you experience a release of energy. This release may be perceived in the body, the mind, the emotions, or all three.

4. Next, think of a concept that you think daily. Some examples are: I am a man/woman; I am hungry; the sky is blue.

5. Divide that thought into smaller and smaller portions and keep dividing until the energy is released. Another way to experience this is to keep withdrawing energy from the thought.

Commentary

At first glance, this meditation appears difficult—especially the second part—because we don't accept that a thing or a thought only exists to the extent that we give it energy. This is like the Zen koan, "What is the sound of a tree falling in the forest with no one there to hear it?" Our intellectual self gives an answer. However, in this meditation we are being asked to make the leap from intellect to our intuitive or sensing nature. Before resisting this meditation, try it!

If you can fully experience this meditation, you will understand how homeopathy works. In homeopathy there is a release of energy when the substance itself no longer exists.

Hint: *Some people find this meditation easier if the division occurs on the breath, so that one takes away half of the substance or thought with each breath.*

WEDNESDAY

Mini-Meditation

What is perceived as gravity is the same energy that draws two lovers to each other.

Meditation

(15 to 20 minutes)

1. Feel the pull of gravity on your body. Imagine that you can make the pull of gravity on your body stronger and weaker at will. When you can feel that ability, move to step two.

2. Imagine that you can feel the pull of gravity on your thoughts. Now imagine you can adjust this pull at will so you can make any thought heavier or lighter.

3. Imagine that you can feel the pull of gravity on your feelings/emotions. Now imagine you can adjust this pull at will so you can make any emotion heavier or lighter.

4. Imagine your body as an entity of light. Feel the pull of gravity on that entity of light until you can make it heavier and lighter at will.

5. Imagine your thoughts as entities of light. Feel the pull of

gravity on those entities of light until you can make them heavier and lighter at will.

6. Imagine your feelings/emotions as entities of light. Feel the pull of gravity on those entities of light until you can make them heavier and lighter at will.

Commentary

This practice demonstrates the force of gravity as it interacts with our thoughts. You may recall that in the sixties, a deep thought was often described as "heavy." Truly the relationship between gravity and our body, mind, and feelings is an outer example of an inner mystery. Gravity is pulling our physical substance towards the center, pulling our thoughts downward towards the center, and even our feelings towards the center. As we learn to counter this force by use of a sense of lightness or weightlessness, we develop more space between thoughts and more space between feelings, and perhaps even more space in the body—if not literally, at least figuratively. Subtle experience needs space. Overcoming the pull of gravity is a wonderful ability that enables us to more effectively control our lives.

Week Four

Meditations on Science and Spirit

THURSDAY

Mini-Meditation

The light of the stars comes from the past to offer us hope for the future.

Meditation

(10 to 12 minutes)

1. Look at a photograph of a starlit sky or a galaxy. Be aware that the stars emitting the starlight might no longer exist. (This is wonderful meditation to do with eyes open, outside on a starry night.)
2. Next, imagine yourself as the light of the stars. See that what you perceive you are is actually what you were.

Commentary

In this meditation, we are exposed to the concept of the
uid nature of time and also the illusory nature of reality in
relation to time. Many of us are still living events that are
long dead, or we are worried about situations that have yet
to be born. A magical release can occur by contemplating
the reality that what we are seeing in the night sky may no
longer be in existence, and yet appears so real.

MEDITATIONS ON SCIENCE AND SPIRIT

FRIDAY

Mini-Meditation

The eye focuses, the mind interprets,
the spirit sees.

Meditation

(5 minutes, and continue to think about the
experience throughout the day)

1. Contemplate your eyeball: only about an inch across, yet able to absorb a hundred miles.

2. The eyeball sees everything in life, but is not able to see itself.

3. The eye is not just an organ of receptivity, but is also an organ of conductivity. (Think about the brightness of the eyes of an infant.)

Commentary

The metaphors here are many. The eyeball is the tool, the mind the interpreter, but who or what actually sees? Even if you figure that out, you still will not be able to see that which does the seeing. And if you get past that koan, you will begin to develop a relationship with the quality of eye-ness or I-ness.

Meditations on Science and Spirit

WEEKEND

Mini-Meditation

What twinkles in the light of the stars is the collective emotion of hope of all humanity.

Meditation
(15 minutes)

1. Make the breath even and gentle in and out through the nose.
2. Look at a picture of the cosmos. Then close your eyes and imagine the cosmos.
3. Imagine your mind being touched by the light of the stars.
4. Imagine focusing the light of the stars in your mind.
5. Imagine that each thought created in your mind is composed of the light of the stars.

6. Imagine your mind filled with the light of the stars. Imagine long periods between thoughts.

Commentary

This meditation, like all meditation on the stars, is really about space and light. Intellectually we are aware that space exists "out there," but most of us relate space only to matter. In this meditation, we diminish the material nature of thought and allow the mind to experience itself in a more subtle way. The key is gentling the breath at the outset. The gentle breath enables us to sense the vacuity of space.

WEEK FIVE

MEDITATIONS ON PEACE

INTRODUCTION

Real peace is a state of body, mind, emotions, heart and soul. It is not stillness but vibration that permeates every part of us. We can be running for a bus and simultaneously be at peace. We can be experiencing a moment of anger and still maintain peace. We can be in deep sorrow and yet be at peace. It is not possible to experience a vibration that is chaotic and maintain peace.

The person who deeply practices meditation will withdraw from the chaotic and find a platform of peace, allowing him/her to transform a chaotic situation into a harmonious one. This applies to our own minds as well as to the situations of life. Peace is a path that must be learned because so much in our outer lives has pulled us away from the path of peace.

The following meditations help activate this place of peace within each of us.

WEEK FIVE

MEDITATIONS ON PEACE

MONDAY

Mini-Meditation

The wind in its fury and the desert in its stillness both represent eternal peace.

Meditation
(10 minutes)

1. With your heart focused on an image of a peaceful lake or ocean, breathe five gentle breaths.
2. With your heart focused on a peaceful forest, breathe five gentle breaths.
3. With your heart focused on a peaceful breeze, breathe five gentle breaths.
4. With your heart focused on a peaceful sound, breathe five gentle breaths.
5. With your heart focused on a windstorm, breathe five gentle breaths.
6. Breathe in and out the heart while thinking the word peace (or shalom, salaam, shanti).

Commentary

Peace is not passivity. Peace is disciplined consciousness moving in a controlled direction. I am indebted to my friend Tai Situ Rinpoche, who coined the phrase "active peace." The experience of peace requires diligent training of the mind and the emotions. Even stormy thoughts can be peaceful, in the presence of a disciplined consciousness. This meditation, though it appears simple, requires repeated application in order to be actually experienced and not merely imagined. That being said, attachment to a goal often promotes restlessness and not peace. Bear in mind that paradox is the signature of the mystical experience.

Week Five

Meditations on Peace

TUESDAY

Mini-Meditation

Divine desires are birthed in the ocean of peace.

Meditation

(7 to 9 minutes)

For each step, the out-breath is natural and relaxed.

1. With each in-breath, imagine you are filling your body with peace. Repeat for fifteen breaths.
2. With each in-breath, imagine you are filling your mind with peace. Repeat for fifteen breaths.
3. With each in-breath, imagine you are filling your heart and feelings with peace. Repeat for fifteen breaths.

Commentary

This is a magical meditation for many of us who live harried lives. It is painfully simple. If you don't have the time for the fifteen breaths, do ten. If you don't have the time for ten, do five. In 45 breaths, the body and the mind are fooled into dropping the weights of the day, and the nectar of peace naturally arises from the heart.

This meditation is good to have in your daily repertoire, and can be done as often as you like, wherever you are. It is not usually suggested that one practice meditation while driving (certainly not with your eyes closed!), but the combination of peace and breath in this practice can be helpful while driving. This also works quite well for children.

MEDITATIONS ON PEACE

WEDNESDAY

Mini-Meditation

There is a peace that exists beyond my sense of self.

Meditation
(9 to 12 minutes)

1. Breathe in and out of the pit of the stomach for twenty breaths. Watch each thought as it arises, as if it is a bubble emerging from the sea of the mind. Allow the thought to dissolve into nothingness.
2. While focusing on the breath, develop some distance between your sense of self and the thoughts. In other words, focus on the breath as self rather than the thoughts as self; identify with the breath, not the thoughts.
3. Experience the mind in the peaceful state.

Commentary

Normally we are not trained to be aware that thinking is just a function of mind. Here we allow the mind's energy to dissolve the unwanted product, in this case thought. Today in our society, the mind is analogous to an insomniac—active all day and active all night. Many people fear losing the ability to think. But controlling the mind actually enhances the ability to concentrate, to think at will, and also to rest the mind at will.

This meditation is quite helpful for people working in professions where much thought and ego are involved daily. It is, in a sense, hatha yoga for the mind.

MEDITATIONS ON PEACE

THURSDAY

Mini-Meditation

When the caterpillar of passion emerges from the cocoon of peacefulness, it becomes the butterfly of love. If there were no caterpillar, there would be no butterfly, and the cocoon would never exist.

Meditation

(maximum 12 minutes)

1. Think of a situation that makes you feel guilty, shameful, sad, grieving, angry, or agitated. (Pick only one.)
2. Imagine that the situation is like a long string that you pull out of your heart.
3. Keep rolling up the string into a ball until it finally ends.
4. Eliminate the string by burying, drowning, or burning it, or turning it to dust.
5. Feel the peace that fills the space taken up by that thought.
6. Transform the feeling of peace to love.

Commentary

Many of the thoughts and feelings that bring so much heaviness and limitation to our lives can be eliminated consciously. Some of us do this through psychotherapy or analysis; some people use bodywork or exercise; some use certain physical postures, as in hatha yoga. Here we are using meditation in a directed way, to intentionally remove negative impressions.

Please note that in step 4 of the instructions, the burying, drowning, burning, or turning to dust corresponds to the four elements: earth, water, fire, and air. As a general guideline, impressions of guilt are best buried; impressions of inferiority, sadness, and grief drowned; excessive passion and anger burned; and impressions caused or held by too much activity in the mind dusted away.

FRIDAY

Mini-Meditation

The fretful sleeper can awaken to a peaceful day as easily as the agitated awakener can fall into a peaceful sleep. Don't assume that the problems of the day lead to problems of the night, or that the peace of the night necessarily leads to the peace of the day.

Meditation

(Create your own time frame for this, but don't overdo it.)

1. Think for a moment of the most looming problem, challenge, or difficulty you are facing in your life.
2. Think of all of the factors that enable this problem.
3. Think of all the solutions that could fix it or change it.
4. Throw all of that away, and imagine that there is no solution to your problem that can originate in the mind. Now place the problem or the challenge in your heart. Breathe in, thinking the word "peace," and breathe out thinking the word "peace." Each time you breathe, feel the problem.
5. Bring peace to the problem and bring the problem to peace.
6. Before you go to sleep tonight, bring peace to the problem

and bring the problem to peace. Upon awakening tomorrow, bring peace to the problem and bring the problem to peace.

7. Continue this meditation until the way you view and relate to the problem changes so that you no longer seek solutions, but instead experience the emotion behind the problem.

8. Relate to the emotion, regardless of what it is, as if it's a spiritual guide directing you home.

Commentary

In life, attitude becomes the controlling factor. Often we see two people with the same life circumstances viewing the situation in exactly opposite ways. This meditation trains us to toss out the purely analytical approach, touch the emotional, and go deeper still to the spiritual.

Meditation is a wonderful guide that leads us into much broader perspectives than those we have become habituated to. Certainly look at a problem in your usual way; but then use your willpower to develop different points of view. For example, we rarely look at problems in an emotional context, in which we ask, "What is the emotional cause of the situation?" Instead we react to problems with our emotions, rather than using our intelligence to find an emotional cause.

This meditation not only helps us find the emotional blockage behind a problem, but also neutralizes some of the emotional charge by using the conscious mind to develop a feeling of peace. In time, we can connect to this feeling of peace at will.

Week Five

Meditations on Peace

WEEKEND

Mini-Meditation

The world is not created for our limitations. Instead, it offers us an opportunity to go beyond our limitations and experience the infinite Creator.

Meditation

(12 to 15 minutes)

1. Using your imagination as a pen, write the word Peace across the soles of your feet. Write in any way or direction you choose. Write as you exhale, not as you inhale.
2. Write the word Peace across the palms of your hands.
3. Write the word Peace across your forehead.
4. Write the word Peace across your back.
5. Write the word Peace across your chest.
6. Write the word Peace across your mind.
7. Write the word Peace across your emotions.
8. Write the word Peace across your soul.

Commentary

Certain words have implicit powers and potentialities within them. By covering the areas of the body, mind, emotions, and soul with the word *Peace* as described in this meditation, we are using our power as human beings to make our lives peaceful at all levels. Note that the vibrations become finer as the meditation progresses.

Some people will be able to do this meditation immediately without any effort. Others might have to struggle for a long period of time. In either case, the end product can be used when needed for the rest of your life.

This is a good meditation to use after long plane rides, confrontations with people, and even before situations that are potentially stressful.

Week Six

Meditations on the Ideal

INTRODUCTION

From childhood onward, human beings learn and grow by aspiring towards an ideal. We idealize actors, sports figures, politicians, authors, and business people, but we reserve our highest adulation for the great servants of humanity. Whether these people are famous or completely unknown, they have overcome self-interest and replaced it with love for their human family. Some are healers, spiritual teachers, awakeners, harmonizers and simple care givers. These are the people who are proud in God rather than proud in ego.

In the following meditations, a visual ideal that represents the greater good found in the depths of every human being is offered as a symbol of concentration. By focusing on the felt sense as well as the visual impression of the different visages, a shift in consciousness will occur. These faces represent a powerful current that runs through human history. As our ideal grows in stature, so does our own being.

Week Six

Meditations on the Ideal

MONDAY

Mini-Meditation

What you give away, you no longer need to carry.

Meditation

(12 to 15 minutes)

1. View the image of the yogi.
2. Close your eyes and imagine the feeling of leaving the world behind, giving away all your worldly possessions, donning a simple garb, and beginning a life of wandering.
3. Imagine yourself as a yogi making a vow of vairagya, or indifference to the outer world. You wander into the high Himalayan Mountains and live in a cave with no comforts except a heightened state of consciousness and complete freedom.
4. Remember your yogic self throughout the day.

Commentary

In the West, we do not have a point of reference that exactly corresponds to this Hindu "loner." A yogi is not a monk in a monastery who lives hidden away from life in the world, but instead is someone who has lived in the outer world and fulfilled his or her responsibilities to family and career, and then has chosen to live a life of solitude in a beautiful, natural surrounding with virtually no material comforts. It is natural for our minds to be at least hesitant and at most repulsed by this idea. How would we eat? How would we deal with the cold or the heat? Where would we sleep? What would we do with the loneliness? The questions are endless.

In this meditation, we are given a chance to experience the freedom of a natural environment without the accustomed support of society. We create an inner cave in our inner mountains to which we can retreat as often as we like, throughout day and night, and experience the state of moksha, or liberation. Most of us will never live in caves. But we can still benefit from removing our minds and emotions from the world outside and retreating within.

Hint: *Don't let your imagination dwell on questions about how your body would feel. Try to imagine the experience of freedom from worldly burdens.*

Week Six

Meditations on the Ideal

TUESDAY

Mini-Meditation

We expand our self by spreading love.

Meditation

(12 to 15 minutes)

1. View the image of the dervish.
2. Close your eyes and imagine the feeling of a being who is consumed by love, a love so powerful that it has gone beyond the object of love and has become Love itself. Experience the power and joy that love without an object creates.
3. Now wander in the bazaar of Istanbul (or some other exotic point in your imagination) and spread love with every step you take.
4. Remember your loving dervish self throughout the day.

Commentary

The dervish is the romantic ideal raised to its highest level—the drunkard intoxicated with the divine wine of love, not just love for God, but love in God. The dervish has lost control in the way that a teenager loses control when experiencing that first deep love. For the dervish, God is not found through limits or rules, but is a beloved whose presence is found in all beings. The dervish does not see you or me, but instead experiences the luminous love and light of God shining through us. Because of that love, the dervish only sees the positive, the hopeful, the deep, and the poignant. The dervish is a being of endless contradictions and paradoxes, resolved only by a love that loves for love's sake alone.

This meditation ultimately becomes a living poem through which we use the mind and emotions to paint a subtle picture. It is in the continual re-creation of this picture that we begin to experience a more intimate relationship with the Divine. It is here that we learn to know God as our lover, not our jailer.

Hint: For this meditation, if you let love lead and reason follow, success is assured.

Week Six

Meditations on the Ideal

WEDNESDAY

Mini-Meditation

The spiritual person's garments
are worn inside out.

Meditation
(12 to 15 minutes)

1. View the image of the Buddhist monk.
2. Close your eyes and imagine the feeling of harmlessness that arises by vowing to act and think no ill will towards any living creature. Imagine that you are living the life of a monk or nun in a Buddhist monastery. Every day is the same routine: predawn meditation emptying the mind, a simple meal eaten with no greed, morning gardening, and the rest of the day spent in meditation and prayer.
3. Leave your monastery and walk into your life here in the world.

Experience the sense of connectedness that having no feeling of harm in your heart toward any creature allows you to feel.

4. Remember your monk or nun throughout the day.

Commentary

Harmlessness is not a value imposed from the outside. Harmlessness is a feeling that naturally arises when we recognize the One Being in all beings. As we begin to have this experience, the Golden Rule becomes a living reality. It's one thing to think that all beings are children of God; it is quite different to actually experience the Oneness behind the multiplicity of faces we encounter in life. In this meditation, do not try to be harmless, but instead, just try to be; and from that state of just being, harmlessness will naturally arise.

(Once you master this meditation, please write to me and let me know how it feels to walk on water.)

Hint: Compare not, criticize not, condemn not, complain not.

THURSDAY

Mini-Meditation

In love, the heart is continually stretched and expanded, sometimes with pain, sometimes with joy.

Meditation
(12 to 15 minutes)

1. View the image of the Christian nun.
2. Close your eyes and imagine you are standing in a field dispensing free food to starving children. They have come to you for sustenance, and you are giving them the feeling of being cared for and loved, a feeling that there is someone who knows they exist. It is your concern, not just the food you offer, that keeps them alive.
3. Stroll through the field, and look into each of their faces; offer love to each one.
4. Remember your nun throughout the day.

Commentary

In all human beings, there is a tendency, latent in some, expressed in others, to accept care and responsibility for the other members of our human family. Often, life drives that tendency so deep within us that it is hidden from our conscious minds. Meditating on the image of a spiritual person whose life fully expresses this sense of responsibility for all can give birth to a similar emotional experience in the one who meditates on it. We experience no release of emotional energy if we think about organizations or governments feeding people because there is no personal contact. But when we meditate on the nun who has dissolved her limited ego in the eternal Christ, who is giving Holy Communion to the suffering children of the world, the experience of heightened spiritual and emotional energy can be profound.

FRIDAY

Mini-Meditation

Give up hope and you give up life.

Meditation
(12 to 15 minutes)

1. View the image of the African healer.
2. Close your eyes and imagine you are living in a small mud and grass hut. The walls are covered with herbs and potions you have gathered and prepared over the years. There are many people waiting outside to see you. All are suffering from some disease of the body or mind. You spend the day feeling the illness, thoughts, and emotions of each one, and allowing their spirit to teach you what word, or touch, or herb, or food they need to heal. To each person, you offer hope and the knowledge that spirit can heal everyone.

3. Now wander through your village and spread the feeling of hope and healing wherever you walk and to each person you encounter.
4. Remember your healer throughout the day.

Commentary

The secret of healing is that it is only effective to a depth equal to that from which the healing comes. Those who heal with the mind reach just below the surface; emotional healers travel deeper still. The real healers are those who experience loss of ego and work from the source of love and consciousness. Often they heal in silence, without any exchange of word or touch with the person to be healed. They allow the spirit or energy of the person to guide the healing so that the wholeness of their being may once again be attained. Many of the great shamans of the past and the present acknowledge that plants and other substances revealed their healing properties while the healer was in a dream state or other very receptive state. It is not our will that heals; it is receiving the energy and love of our own spirit and commingling that with the energy and love of all to whom we minister.

Hint: Don't be distracted by the symptoms of illness, regardless of how terrible they may appear. The first act of healing is covering the wounds of others from our own sight.

WEEK SIX

MEDITATIONS ON THE IDEAL

WEEKEND

Mini-Meditation

*Our lives are like a little child with a secret,
bursting to share it and give it forth, yet at
the same time knowing it must be kept within.
As the smallest atom releases vast quantities
of energy when its core is touched, the core of
the human is waiting to open its storehouse.*

Meditation

(12 to 15 minutes)

1. In your mind's mirror, view the image of yourself.
2. See yourself cleaning wounds on the eaten limbs of a leper in Calcutta or feeding a starving infant in central Africa or calming a psychotic old woman in a New York hospital. See yourself washing the feet of any human being who suffers anywhere in the world. Feel what it is like to serve humanity.
3. Now wander through your home or your office, through your classroom or neighborhood, and spread the presence of service wherever you walk and to each person you encounter.
4. Remember your saintly self throughout the day.

Commentary

This can either be a wonderful meditation or a terrible meditation. If you focus on yourself, this will be a difficult experience. If you can efface yourself in those whom you serve, the experience is very self-nurturing. It is admittedly difficult, even mentally, to perform the actions described above. However, this meditation softens the wall of fear and separation that creates the difficulty. If your focus is on pain and suffering, that is what will be sustained. If your focus is on service, the removal of pain and suffering will naturally occur. The challenge in this meditation comes when we travel from our own minds to those we actually encounter in the world. You need not bathe the leper, but instead symbolically bathe and serve the one who cuts you off in traffic. You might not feed the starving infant, but certainly you can feed those who are starving for a smile or a friendly gesture. Whomever you serve, when you act from an awakened heart, the whole universe benefits and responds.

Hint: This is a perfume-like meditation. It's subtle. You need to sense the nuance of the practice rather than see its details.

Week Seven

Planetary Meditations

INTRODUCTION

Expanding the relationship between our hearts and minds and the planets is an allegory for experiencing the relationship between spirit and the various aspects of our personalities. If the planets in these meditations are viewed as symbolic keys to open us to a deeper understanding of ourselves, then these meditations will have an enlightening effect.

I have met hardened scientists working on space travel and exploration who sub-consciously ascribe personality attributes to the planets. Without arguing for or against the efficacy of astrology, I must admit having incredibly beautiful meditations sitting outside on a summer night and focusing on one or another of these heavenly bodies. They did each seem to have a unique consciousness that was both visceral and mentally stimulating.

These meditations are designed to foster a relationship with the planets.

Week Seven

Planetary Meditations

MONDAY

Mini-Meditation

Mercury is the energy of communication and short-term accomplishment.

Meditation

(4 to 5 minutes)

1. Attune to the planet Mercury by breathing through the nose very rapidly for about twenty seconds.
2. Open your eyes, keep the breath rapid, and focus your attention on any object in the room or out the window. Hold your gaze for about five seconds and move to a new object.
3. Repeat for five objects, then breathe naturally.
4. Without thinking (too much), fill in the blanks in the list below. Try to have the answers relate to your everyday outer life.

      I want _____

      I need _____

      I hope _____

      I feel _____

Commentary

It is wise to remember in this meditation that Mercury, the planet closest to the sun, is pictured as the messenger of the light of the sun. Mercury is closely associated with the mind, which the ancients believed was the communication facilitator for the light of the heart. By following the breathing exercise suggested above and accelerating the breath, we are replicating a certain rhythm that is more conducive to communicating than it is to creating. When the meditator fills in the five blanks, what is communicated, ideally, is the needs and desires of the heart rather than the mind. This is a wonderful meditation for writers, salespeople, clergy, and schoolteachers.

WEEK SEVEN

PLANETARY MEDITATIONS

TUESDAY

Mini-Meditation

Venus is the creator, appreciator, and harmonizer of all of life with beauty.

Meditation

(10 minutes)

1. Attune to the planet Venus by taking several concentrated in-breaths through the left nostril. Relax and exhale naturally through both nostrils.

2. Bathe your body and mind in a beautiful color. Allow your body and mind to dissolve in that color.

3. Wash your body and mind in a beautiful sound (like HU or AH or MM). Allow your body and mind to dissolve in that sound.

4. Now crush your body and mind with beautiful gems. Allow your body and mind to dissolve in that sensation.

5. Caress your body and mind with a beautiful scent. Allow your body and mind to dissolve in that scent.

6. Suggest to yourself that beauty will arise gracefully from your body and mind.

Commentary

In this meditation, we are attuning to the planet Venus and the attribute of beauty by using the doorways of the senses. This technique was used by the ancients to discipline the imagination and direct the consciousness inward. When we imagine beauty, we are usually rewarded by a natural sense or feeling of beauty that emerges when the visualization ends. Mystics often say that love manifests as beauty; or, in other words, God is beautiful and loves beauty. In a society that does not emphasize natural beauty, any attempt to rekindle the connection with that natural beauty is appreciated by the spirit.

WEDNESDAY

Mini-Meditation

Mars is the power of the collectivity, the joy of restraint, and the energy of victory.

Meditation

(10 minutes)

1. Attune to the planet Mars by taking several strong in-breaths through the right nostril. Relax and exhale reflexively through both nostrils.

2. Replicate yourself into forty identical beings—forty bodies, forty minds, forty emotional vehicles, and so on.

3. Have all forty stand in formation so that there are ten rows of four, forming a rectangle.

4. March the rectangle forward for ten steps. Now march it to the right for ten steps. Do an about-face and march in the other directions for ten steps. Turn and go forward again for ten steps.

5. Allow any impulse that wishes to break the formation to be dissolved by the steady cadence of the marching steps of the group. Allow any impulse that is repulsed by the

uniformity of the group to see its mirror image, which is a certain ease at being an accepted part of the formation.

6. Maintain a steady rhythm and keep marching forward, not just with the body, but with the mind, the emotions, and the spirit, all moving in a unified form.

7. Draw the forty separate beings back into yourself and feel the full power of your one being.

Commentary

Before you spend the entire day trying to divide your consciousness into exactly forty marching soldiers, try instead to create a group of approximately forty. The intention here is not necessarily to get the exact count, but to get the feel of being a militaristic unit with many parts, all identical. What makes this meditation work is the inner sound or rhythm of marching. By attuning to the planet Mars in meditation, we can improve our inner discipline and also knock some of the feistiness out of our false ego or limited self.

Hint: Humming one of John Philip Sousa's marches silently or aloud while doing this meditation will help greatly. If you are too self-conscious, at least beat out a marching rhythm on your desktop or meditation stool to put yourself in the groove.

THURSDAY

Mini-Meditation

Jupiter is the force of expansion,
sovereignty, and breadth rather than depth.

Meditation

(5 to 7 minutes)

1. This meditation is best done standing, out-of-doors or looking out a window. Attune to the planet Jupiter by taking several very full, deep breaths through both nostrils. Hold the breath for a few moments on each inhalation and feel the expansion in your being.

2. Look at the horizon and ask yourself, "What do I own between the point of my body and the horizon?" Answer the question with "I own everything."

3. Now imagine that you can extend your energy 100 miles beyond the horizon and ask yourself, "What do I own between here and the 100 miles past the horizon?" Answer the question with "I own everything."

4. Now imagine that you can extend your energy 1000 miles beyond the horizon and ask yourself, "What do I own between here and the 1000 miles past the horizon?"

Answer the question with "I own everything."

5. With the feeling of being the ruler of this vast domain, walk through the domain in an almost egocentric state and feel, "I am responsible for all that I see, all that I think, and all that I feel." See how your being is the focal point of all beings in your domain, how you are the ruler of all beings in your domain.

6. Allow the domain and yourself to expand beyond any finite limit.

Commentary

Certainly one can see the danger of feeding the false ego if this meditation is done solely on the mind or personal level. The intention, however, is to awaken a feeling of vastness and absence of boundaries. Our concepts of space and distance are defined by the size of our planet. However, as people begin to experience inner space, they are often shocked by the hugeness. This meditation pulls us out of the "tempest in our teacup" and allows for the natural development of a much greater perspective. If at the end of this meditation you think about the problems in your life, they might seem small and tri ing.

FRIDAY

Mini-Meditation

*Saturn is the power of slowness, the
wisdom of age, and the knowledge
that comes with experience.*

Meditation
(10 minutes)

1. Attune to the planet Saturn by breathing slowly though
   the nose, concentrating your energy on the long, slow
   exhalation.
2. Slow down the processes of your mind. Slow down the
   processes of your body. Slow down the processes of your
   breath.
3. Rotate your head in a clockwise manner for approximately ten or fifteen full circles by moving your chin towards
   your left shoulder, then the sternum, the right shoulder,
   then the ceiling or the sky.
4. Feel the part of the ego that judges what you do, think,
   and feel.

5. Feel the part of the ego that is always imagining what others think of you.
6. Experience that what appears in you as a judge and a critic is, at its core, a profound force to keep you pure and deep.
7. Feel the clarity of pure discrimination without judgment.

Commentary

By slowing down the rhythm of the mind, we can change the self-critical habit to a more productive, intuitive self-analysis. Saturn offers us an opportunity to see the aspect of the ego that imprisons us with self-doubt. We transform the seed of discrimination into the weed of inferiority by mistakenly allowing discernment to devolve into lack of self-confidence. This meditation creates a natural garden for that seed to grow into wisdom and perception instead of self-doubt. Some people may find meditating on Saturn to be heavy and depressing, but if your nature is deep and serious, this meditation can transport you to a place of peace and protection. This meditation is also helpful for people who have very impulsive minds.

There is benefit in learning to experience the different aspects of mind that function in a habitual way, and to observe how we lump together all of those different functions of mind and call that lump "me."

PLANETARY MEDITATIONS

WEEKEND

Mini-Meditation

Planets, stars, galaxies, black holes, seemingly empty space... all are waiting to be asked to dance.

Meditation
(15 minutes)

1. Breathe in and out the nose. Attune the breath to space by experiencing as refined a breath as you are able to perform. Try to make the breath finer and softer with each inhalation and exhalation until you begin to draw in energy from space itself. (Be careful not to let yourself feel faint or suffocated. If this begins to happen, breathe more deeply until the condition passes.)

2. Notice the quality of life that is pervasive throughout space. Bring that directionless energy into your heart, mind, and body.

3. Let the energy of space remove any burden from your heart.

4. Let the energy of space lighten the density of thought and create energy-giving voids between each thought.

5. Draw the energy of space into the physical body. Envision the stars, the planets, and the human body emerging out of the infinite energy of life in space.

Commentary

The key to this meditation is given in the second section, where the energy of space is described as being directionless. In life we have been trained to give everything direction, whether it is linear or circular. Space takes direction only when objects are placed in it. Of course not only physical objects, but thoughts and concepts can also give space direction. But when we take out landmarks, when we remove the center of space, when we begin to experience space as all-pervading, then we actually feel the true nature of space. In this meditation, use your willpower and a very refined breath to actually experience space rather than your concept of space.

WEEK EIGHT

MEDITATIONS ON ATTRIBUTES

INTRODUCTION

When asked to describe a person, place, or thing, we often respond by listing attributes. They might be physical, they might be emotional, they might be fanciful, but the common ground is that they are all attributes. For example, every human being has a nose, but we often ascribe attributes such as size or shape which help us to describe and thereby know it.

In meditation, the use of attributes is very important. We aim to know that which is universal in all of us by experiencing the attributes which are found to greater or lesser degrees in each human being. By focusing our attention on these attributes, we enhance them.

The following meditations focus our consciousness on the attributes within us that are directly relevant to the way we view and experience life. By focusing on them, we make them knowable, stronger and relevant. As we make the universe a reality in our lives, it makes us an awakened part of itself.

MEDITATIONS ON ATTRIBUTES

MONDAY

Mini-Meditation

Truth is the human spirit unfettered by
limited desire.

Meditation
(7 to 10 minutes)

1. Imagine truth as a visceral sensation that dawns in the depth of the solar plexus/heart and expands throughout the body, mind, and feelings. This truth is an absolute without opposite. No falsehood can exist in the presence of truth. Imagine truth as a powerful light that makes known that which is hidden. The light has no self-interest. It illumines everything it touches.
2. Bring whatever doubts or fears or hopes you feel to stand before the light of truth.
3. Bring a problem or a dilemma before the light of truth—either the issue from step two or a new one—and experience what it's like to come away with illumination rather than with an answer.

Commentary

Writing about truth with words is a sure way to miss it. Truth emerges from the deep, the silent, the still, and the eternal. In some religions, the word for God translates as truth rather than deity. In this practice, we emphasize what is sensed, intuited, felt, and perceived, in order to experience truth rather than our concepts of truth. Many of us are not accustomed to using these more subtle modes of perception, and to do so requires self-training. I could suggest that each of us go outside and stare at the clouds for a while, or the light of the moon, or even our own navels, as some practitioners have urged. But I believe it is more powerful to find the equivalent of these mind-stilling events in our own lives.

It is almost universally accepted that observing and calming the breath leads to a heightening of the subtle faculties. In the Heart of Perfect Wisdom Sutra, there is a wonderful phrase referring to a great mantra, or spiritual teaching. The Buddha calls this mantra "True because not false." In other words, there is no falseness, apparent or hidden, anywhere in this mantra. For the above meditation, find the place that is true because not false.

Week Eight

Meditations on Attributes

Tuesday

Mini-Meditation

All battles in life ultimately lead to the victory over the limited self. Some lose many battles so that the final victory will have the perfume of sweetness and innocence.

Meditation
(7 to 10 minutes)

1. Imagine victory as a visceral sensation that begins in the feet and slowly rises through the entire body. Try to experience victory as a sense of the true self, rather than the energy of conquering anything outside of us.
2. Practice breathing with a sense of victory. Bring before the power of victory whatever fears, defeats, or limitations you experience habitually. Allow the light of victory to shine upon those limitations.
3. Breathe in and think, "I am." Breathe out and think, "victorious."

Commentary

Initially, it is a stretch of the imagination to conceive of victory without an enemy or situation to overcome. However, by learning to experience victory without opposition, we remove all energy from opposition and incorporate that energy quite naturally into victory. Certainly the general on the battlefield facing 100,000 enemy troops will have difficulty in not seeing opposition. But victory actually occurs in the moment when the thought and fear of defeat disappear and are replaced by certainty and stillness.

How many times in history have we heard of a small group of ill-equipped warriors defeating a seemingly much more powerful and numerous force? The small group, or maybe even only their leader, has come to experience the inner state of balance and detachment that manifests outwardly as the necessary concentration of energy that, combined with an ample dose of wisdom, experience, and inspiration, must lead to victory. Without the above experience in our lives, we may win some battles, but lose the war. If we don't develop detachment with victory, our attachment to victory often leads to our defeat.

WEEK EIGHT

MEDITATIONS ON ATTRIBUTES

WEDNESDAY

Mini-Meditation

Compassion is neither defined nor limited by the individual struggles we experience in life. These are merely stations that transform us into compassionate human beings.

Meditation
(7 to 10 minutes)

1. Imagine compassion as a visceral feeling that begins in the heart and touches all of the body and mind. This is an absolute feeling of compassion, not rooted in guilt nor in a desire to do good. This is a natural state of caring.

2. Allow your heart-mind to bring before itself the image or the name of some people who have wronged you. Feel this absolute compassion as it flows over both you and them. Breathe in caring and breathe out forgiveness while sensing the absolute nature of compassion.

Commentary

We can no more try to be compassionate than we can try to be loving. These states so represent the very core of our being that the only skill we can develop is the ability to remove the artifice of our personalities that stands between the compassion at our core and the expression of that compassion outwardly in the world. This does not mean that we remove the personality. Instead, in this meditation, we remind the personality of the experience of acting from that core attribute without the cautions and self-consciousness that life has taught us.

When an infant is born, the love and light that freely pours from its eyes and smile shines on all human beings, regardless of whether they wish to nurture or harm the infant. In many spiritual teachings, compassion is equated with rain that falls on all beings. It is relatively easy to be compassionate with those we love and respect. This meditation teaches true compassion, which is offered where it is needed rather than where it is easy. Of course the decision of need is removed from our scope by the inner training we give ourselves to allow that compassion to ow freely on all.

Hint: Do not go to step two until you have mastered step one.

WEEK EIGHT

MEDITATIONS ON ATTRIBUTES

THURSDAY

Mini-Meditation

One cannot be healthy and limited at the same time. The great sages of humanity are healthy even if their bodies experience disease, and the unawakened ones are not healthy even if there is no apparent disease in the body.

Meditation
(7 to 10 minutes)

1. Imagine a feeling of health as a visceral sensation that begins in the palms of the hands and the soles of the feet and moves toward the core of the body and mind. Feel this health as a state of balance between the below and the above, the right and the left, the in-ness and the out-ness, all meeting in the center.
2. Breathe the thought of healing in and the thought of health out. As you breathe, sense any imbalance between the right and the left, the above and below, the within and without, and bring them to an absolute state of balance. Imagine your being as timeless and boundless, while simultaneously maintaining a balanced experience of time and space.

3. Fill all the spaces of your mind and emotions with profound health.

Commentary

The lesson of this meditation is the equation of health with balance. Disease of any kind is a manifestation of some imbalance. Therefore, in order to promote health, we must train ourselves to promote balance. Many years ago, I was involved in a seminar about business. One of the speakers suggested that corporations should strive to earn a balanced profit as opposed to earning a huge profit. His thesis was that if the profit becomes too large, there is often a dangerous tendency towards unbalanced growth, leading to tragic consequences. In a sense, the same is true with our health. If we eat some food, we feel satisfied. If we eat too much food, we feel sick. The examples are endless. The point in this meditation is to experience health and balance at a level much deeper and much higher than the habits we've developed in life. As we meditate on this condition, the outer, unbalanced habits will begin to fall away. It is never too late to practice balance.

This meditation has a wonderful interplay between the absolute and the relative. That interplay has been incorporated in all of the world's religions and many philosophies. In religion, prayer and meditation represent the absolute, and righteous living represents the relative. Each naturally leads to the other.

FRIDAY

Mini-Meditation

Science today is reaching the very end of the long road of matter. It will find there the beginning of the path of vibration.

Meditation
(7 to 10 minutes)

1. Imagine pure vibration that begins in the timeless and directionless essence of your being and touches your feeling, your thought, and your body. Whatever feeling or thought comes to you, immediately dissolve it in the subtle power of pure vibration.
2. Sense the absolute vibration behind all the activity of life. Sense the vibration at the very core of planet Earth, in the very essence of the sun, and in the emptiness of space. Feel the all-pervading nature of vibration.
3. Bring the limited sense of your body and ego to stand before the limitless nature of vibration. Imagine vibration in a state before it was perceived.

Commentary

The entire process of creation, pre-creation, and post-creation can be described as "stillness to vibration to stillness." If the Absolute is stillness, the movement of that stillness produces form, which then dissolves back to stillness. Vibration is the word we use to connote movement. Because everything is vibration, vibration can dissolve everything. When vibration takes form, we say it is thought or feeling or object. But it is possible to experience pure vibration. If we concentrate on silence, then sound (usually inner sound) will emerge. When the mystics wish to hear these inner sounds in meditation, they cover their ears so the inner silence can be heard.

WEEKEND

Mini-Meditation

Life begins with an impulse upwards toward the surface, and develops meaningfulness by turning inward.

Meditation

(7 minutes)

1. Feel the energy of gravity, which the mystics know to be the energy of constraint. Imagine the energy of eternal constraint. Visualize a black hole in outer space, with a force of constraint so powerful it pulls the energy of light into its own center.

2. The mind wants to go either through or around constraint, but for this moment see constraint as a force that can magnify the essential energy of your being by not letting it emerge in any direction.

3. Draw toward your center the energy found in the breath, thought, and feeling. Our impulse is to attach these energies to objects, but for this meditation let every feeling

and thought draw you to your core. Practice restraining the mind and the emotions.

Commentary

The reactive part of our personality often does not feel comfortable with constraint. In this meditation, we train ourselves to use the pull at the center of our body/mind/heart, to focus our essential energy. Think of this meditation as isometric exercise: the force is there without the movement. As we resist the energy to expand outward, the constrained energy moves inward. This process directs our consciousness to our core being, which enables us to experience life in a more peaceful condition.

WEEK NINE

MEDITATIONS ON OPPOSITES

INTRODUCTION

An important characteristic of the way people learn is by experiencing opposites, and often the opposites create duality rather than promoting a unified viewpoint of life. Some people like hot weather and some people like cold, for example. And as soon as we develop a preference towards one or the other, we invest in that choice at the expense of its opposite. Suddenly our preference becomes our team, and we root for it in hopes that it will be victorious. If it was up to the hot weather people the world would be 80 degrees, whereas the cold weather people would be wishing for ice and snow.

For the journeyer on the path of meditation, learning from the dynamic of the opposites, rather than choosing one over the other, lifts the mind and intelligence towards unity. Unifying opposites also trains the critical mind to give up attachment to one point of view and become more open to many. These meditations, if practiced regularly, will benefit you by softening the judgmental nature of your mind and enhancing your intuitive gifts.

WEEK NINE

MEDITATIONS ON OPPOSITES

MONDAY

Mini-Meditation

The first impulse arises to meet the last moment of rest.

Alpha/Omega Meditation
(7 to 10 minutes)

1. With each in-breath and out-breath, imagine you are traveling backwards through your own lifetime. If you are under thirty, regress three years at a time. If you are 31 or older, regress five years at a time. Spend at least three breaths feeling each three- or five-year period. Continue traveling backwards until you are breathing in the period that corresponds to your earliest childhood.

2. When you reach this time period, continue breathing for ten full breaths. Allow each breath to draw you back to the first breath of your life. Holding the sensation that you are taking the first breath of your life, breathe without counting for a minute or so.

3. Now imagine that you are breathing the last breath of your life. Holding the sensation that you are taking in

and releasing the last breath of your life, breathe without counting for a minute or so.

4. Sense the relationship between the first breaths and the last breaths. See the breaths as a wheel rather than a line, and experience the circularity of the cycle. Any given point on the wheel can be first and/or last. If you wish, breathe in and think "the first," and breathe out and think "the last."

Commentary

Mystics often use opposites to remove their consciousness from the world of opposites. They see birth and death as different moments of the same experience. Every beginning has its end potentially within it; and every ending sprouts a potential new beginning. This meditation functions on many different levels. Seeing life as a wheel can be a new point of view, as can seeing opposites as one, or seeing the cyclical nature and relationship of infancy and old age.

Hint: The more courage you bring to this meditation, the more profound the results. Do not fear imagining your last breaths, as the acceptance of death leads to the knowledge that death holds as a secret.

Week Nine

Meditations on Opposites

TUESDAY

Mini-Meditation

We create to express our soul's potentials.
We destroy to remove the obstacles on the
path to fulfillment.

Creative/Destructive Meditation
(7 to 10 minutes)

1. Make the breath slightly stronger than normal for both the inhalation and the exhalation. Now use your breath to find the energy that creates. Don't look for the fruits of the creation, but instead sense the pure energy of creation.
2. In your imagination, create something that is positive for your life, and then feel it dissolve.
3. Create something that is negative for your life, and then dissolve that.
4. Now create something that is fearful, and dissolve that.
5. Create something that is doubtful, and dissolve that.
6. Create any thought at all, and dissolve that thought.
7. Now take the energy of dissolution and destruction and turn that into creativity. As you exhale, feel dissolution

and destruction. As you inhale, feel creation. Note how with each full breath we both create and destroy. As you breathe in, think the word "create." As you breathe out, think "destroy."

Commentary

Many of us have grown up with the concept that creation is good and dissolution or destruction bad. The outcome of this is a tendency to hold on to all that we have created. We have not been taught how to consciously dissolve or destroy that which is finished in our lives or minds. This meditation gives us practice in wisely using the power to dissolve as a positive force in our lives. Imagine the freedom you can experience from the tyranny of your own mind if you can dissolve thoughts and feelings at will.

Hint: This meditation is reinforced by practice. Throughout your days, consciously remove and destroy thoughts and tendencies that have run their course. Even the simple act of giving away one of our possessions helps us strengthen this force.

WEDNESDAY

Mini-Meditation

Life limits us so that we can know its detail and exalts us so that we are able to experience its vastness.

Abase/Exalt Meditation

(7 to 10 minutes)

1. Imagine life as limited in every direction. Whatever you do is stopped and crumbles. Your broad mind becomes narrow, your feeling heart stops feeling, your high ideals disappear. Every direction presents a wall that limits you and makes you feel small. Without attachment, feel the energy of this limitation. Without making a judgment of good or bad, observe how the mind can drag you down.

2. Now be aware of the opposite—how you as an individual can be raised to a most exalted position. See yourself as the queen or the king, the wise teacher, the great artist, the loving, limitless human being.

3. As you inhale, be aware of yourself being limited and

pulled down, and as you exhale, feel yourself being exalted, limitless, and elevated.

4. See if you can experience the energy of being abased or limited without imagining personal examples. See if you can experience the energy of exaltation without personalizing. By making no judgment on either, one can fully experience both.

Commentary

This meditation is only for the very brave. If you have no desire to do this meditation, just move on without feeling any judgment. Some people ask, "What is the purpose of this meditation?" It is a powerful tool in developing detachment. Unless we experience the power that can drag us down as well as uplift us, there is a tendency to base our spiritual lives on our own needs and expectations, rather than on the full creative force of the universe. If we are dragged down, it is a wonderful opportunity to develop mastery and fearlessness. If we are raised high, it is time to develop gratitude and generosity.

THURSDAY

Mini-Meditation

Expansion moves love in every direction.
Contraction draws universal love
into a single point.

Expand/Contract Meditation
(15 minutes)

1. With each inhalation, imagine your body is getting bigger and bigger. Do this ten times, focusing on the inhalation and the expansion.

2. Now focus on the exhalation, and allow the body to become smaller and smaller. With each exhalation, contract the body until it diminishes to a single point. Do this ten times.

3. With each inhalation, imagine your mind is getting bigger and bigger. Do this ten times, focusing on the inhalation and the expansion.

4. Now focus on the exhalation, contracting the mind until it has diminished to a single point of thought. Do this for ten breaths.

5. For ten breaths, imagine your emotions are expanding, focusing on the inhalation and the expansion.

6. For the next ten breaths, focus on the exhalation, con-

tracting the emotions to a single point.

7. For ten breaths, expand the spirit, focusing on the inhalation and the expansion.

8. For ten breaths focus on the exhalation, contracting the spirit to a single point.

Commentary

The ability to expand and contract mind and emotion is a great aid to daily life in this complex world. Some situations seem terribly weighty until we can expand our minds and see that they really are a tempest in a teacup. If we say to someone, "Don't be so troubled about such a small matter," often it does not have a positive effect, and it can fix the person's mind or emotions on the situation. However, sharing with people how to expand consciousness, so they can sit in the vast space of mind or feeling, will naturally enable them to gain clear perspective.

The expansion and the contraction of the spirit is quite a different matter. The expansion in this case allows us to experience the oneness in the many forms. The contraction emphasizes the source and the goal. In time, you can journey in spirit from an experience of oneness to an experience of diversity and back again throughout the day. Experiencing these two states of the spirit helps us touch the goal of life, which is balance. The number of times we traverse from the source to the many depends upon our ability to maintain a focus on the One in all circumstances of life.

FRIDAY

Mini-Meditation

In the awakened one, the wrathful face masks the peaceful spirit. In the unawakened one, often the peaceful face masks a wrathful spirit.

Wrathful/Peaceful Meditation

(10 minutes)

1. Use your creative powers to construct a mythological, wrathful being. Use your imagination and your deep instincts to imbue this being with as much detail as possible. This being is full of fire and power, and through that wrathfulness destroys any blockage in your being or any part of you that deviates from the truth. Allow this wrathful being to uproot all thoughts of doubt, self-pity, or fear within you.

2. Use your creative powers to construct a mythological being of peace and tranquility. Imagine that this being has stillness and depth, and that all activity in your being

is absorbed in its peacefulness, so only stillness remains. Allow this being to dissolve any agitation or need for excitement within you.

Commentary

We have a tendency to categorize wrathful beings as those on the side of darkness or ill will. This meditation helps us to use both the wrathful and the peaceful sides of creation as opposite energies that produce positive effects. A great lesson is learned when you can place the mask of wrathfulness on yourself and, by the power of your glance, shake off those unclear impressions and thoughts that stick to you. In the same way, you can create a mythological being of peace that dissolves chaotic thoughts and feelings in an ocean of stillness.

Meditations on Opposites

WEEKEND

Mini-Meditation

The cup must be emptied before it can be cleaned and filled again. It is difficult to wash a cup when it is full of wine.

Empty/Full Meditation

(20 minutes)

1. Imagine your skin as a vessel that is filled with the rest of your physical body—bones, blood, organs, esh, and neural matter. As you exhale, imagine that someone has pulled the plug from the soles of your feet, and all of the physical matter of your body drains out. Do this for fifteen breaths, until you experience your skin as an empty vessel.

2. For the next fifteen breaths, as you inhale, imagine that you are consciously filling the vessel with all of your inner ingredients, which have been purified by their journey outside of the skin. On each inhalation, bring in your purified bones, blood, organs, esh, and neural matter.

3. Now imagine your mind as a bowl made of thought matter, the interior of which is filled with your thoughts.

As you exhale, allow the bowl to become progressively empty of all thoughts. Do this for fifteen breaths, until you experience the mind as an empty bowl.

4. For the next fifteen breaths, as you inhale, fill the mind with purified thought matter.

5. Now imagine your feelings and emotions to be clothed in diaphanous gauze. As you exhale, allow all feelings to be pulled from the gauze until the fabric wafts gently in the breeze. Do this for fifteen breaths, until you experience your emotional body as a sheer, empty garment.

6. For the next fifteen breaths, as you inhale, draw in the refined energy of feeling that naturally clings to the emotional gauze, enhancing rather than blocking it.

Commentary

In this meditation, we are using opposites to purify and recharge. When we allow the body, the mind, the emotions to empty, whatever is unclean or dense will naturally fall away. As we draw the forms back into us, they feel revivified by having been emptied and made whole again. As you exhale, do not hold anything back. Use your will as the fuel to make sure that all parts of the body, all thought, and all feeling is fully put out of your self.

With a bit of training, you will be able to empty body, mind, and feelings at will as the situation needs.

MEDITATIONS ON SOUND

INTRODUCTION

The format this week will differ from other weeks in that these meditations require you to produce a sound and to use that sound for inner awakening. If you are in an environment where you cannot comfortably voice the sound, you can use your imagination to inwardly create the sound. However, it is more effective to actually make the physical sound.

In making the sound aloud, don't be concerned with proper pronunciation, but instead with listening to whatever sound is produced. It is also important to place the vibration of the sound in the area of the body as directed. For some this will be an actual physical experience, for others a subtle, ethereal experience. The emphasis must be on experiencing rather than expectation or desire to "get it right."

Cautions: These exercises are not to be done while driving. The weekend practice is best done at home in quiet. If you feel dizzy or lightheaded, stop wherever you are in the cycle, breathe a little deeper, and when comfortable, begin again, shortening the time that you hold each sound.

The goal is not necessarily to do the full number of repetitions, as if you were lifting weights, but rather to experience moments of transformative energy. In this series of meditations, the person who is deeply affected after two or three repetitions gains greatly, whereas the person who pushes to complete the prescribed number might be only strengthening the ego. A very delicate balance between sensitivity and will power is necessary.

You can find audio demonstrations of meditations in this book, as well as additional resources, at www.UniversalMeditations.com.

MONDAY

Mini-Meditation

The loving nature, although more sensitive to the pains of this world, is more closely attuned to the next world.

Meditation

(6 to 8 minutes)

1. Using your natural voice, intone the syllable "ka" twenty times, holding each repetition for three or four seconds. Try to place the vibration of the sound behind the sternum in the center of the chest.
2. Switch to the syllable "ga" and repeat the exercise as above.
3. Repeat the above cycle, saying first "ka," then "ga," another twenty times each.
4. Finally, intone the syllable "la" forty times. Continue to place the vibration in the center of the chest and hold each repetition for three or four seconds.
5. Allow yourself to feel loving as you do this meditation.

Commentary

These sounds will foster the opening of the heart center. As you focus on the "ah" sound in each syllable, try to imagine the sound emerging from the center of the chest rather than from the mouth. See yourself pushing the sound down into the heart center, rather than lifting it up into the head. At first, the feeling might be artificial and strained, but if you persist, a feeling of openness will be produced. For those who have never done practices with sound, there might be a tendency to be self-conscious at first. The solution, of course, is persistence and focusing on the sound regardless of the state of the ego. Remembering the guidance to feel loving is very helpful for this meditation.

You can find audio demonstrations of meditations in this book, as well as additional resources, at www.UniversalMeditations.com.

MEDITATIONS ON SOUND

TUESDAY

Mini-Meditation

*The energy of awakening pierces
the armor of duality.*

Meditation

(10 minutes)

1. Using your natural voice, intone the sound "huiee" forty times, holding each repetition for 3 seconds. Feel the vibration of the sound in the center of the forehead.
2. Intone the syllable "la" forty times, placing the vibration of the sound in the center of the chest.
3. Return to the sound "huiee," vibrating in the forehead, for eighty repetitions. (If you do not have time to complete eighty, do forty.)
4. The feeling of this exercise is piercing.

Commentary

In this meditation, we begin to sensitize what has been popularly called "the third eye." This is the main seat of insight, and as it opens, our perception of people and events will deepen. We are purposely emphasizing the connection between the heart and the third eye, as the heart is the source of all the centers. It is true that the base of the spine is a great repository of energy, but the heart's reservoir is infinitely more vast.

You can find audio demonstrations of meditations in this book, as well as additional resources, at www.UniversalMeditations.com.

WEEK TEN

MEDITATIONS ON SOUND

WEDNESDAY

Mini-Meditation

*Awaken now or awaken later, it's no matter,
for awaken you must.*

Meditation

(8 minutes)

1. Imagine a straight line drawn from the top of your head to the back of your tongue, and another drawn through the head from ear to ear. Now imagine a golf-ball-sized space where the two lines intersect.
2. Using your natural voice, make the sound "ong" fifteen times, placing the vibration in the space described above. Hold the sound on "ng" rather than the opening "ah" sound, and hold each repetition for four seconds.
3. Intone the sound "huiee" ten times, placing the vibration in the center of the forehead.
4. Repeat the above cycle twice more (fifteen ongs, ten huiees, fifteen ongs, ten huiees.)
5. The feeling is one of awakening.

Commentary

The sound "huiee" corresponds to the surface of the third eye, the sound "ong" to the depth of the third eye. As you make these sounds, imagine the atmosphere around your head to be very clean and clear. Do not be surprised or alarmed if these sounds produce inner visual experiences. It is not unusual to see colors or light within. Remember, we all have different inborn qualities and levels of sensitivity, which enable us to best express our natures.

You can find audio demonstrations of meditations in this book, as well as additional resources, at www.UniversalMeditations.com.

Week Ten

Meditations on Sound

THURSDAY

Mini-Meditation

For lovers, the horizon is infinite, and they are constantly striving to reach it.

Meditation

(10 to 15 minutes)

1. Using your natural voice, intone the syllable "dom" (to rhyme with "mom") fifty times, holding each repetition for three seconds. The sound should feel as if it is coming from the lower back.
2. Now intone the syllable "som" (also rhyming with "mom") fifty times, again holding each repetition for three seconds. The sound should feel as if it is coming from the shoulder blades and the upper back.
3. Repeat the cycle up to twice more if you wish.
4. The feeling is extending and expanding.

Commentary

Traditionally, the back is the larger expression of the heart center. The lower back exchanges energy and impressions with our outer life, the upper back with our inner, more mystical part. Many people who are having difficulty in life experience pain in the lower back, for which there is a plethora of self-help books. However, it is not just physical exercise, but also the exercise of vibrations that helps the lower back survive the sometimes crushing nature of life in the world.

The upper back is the home to inner doubts and fears of being excluded. The vibratory effect of this practice will help unwind these doubts and fears if done on a daily basis.

The message of the Mini-Meditation is the recognition that some pain is an integral part of life in this world. However, part of our duty as loving human beings is to remove unnecessary pain in others and in ourselves.

You can find audio demonstrations of meditations in this book, as well as additional resources, at www.UniversalMeditations.com.

FRIDAY

Mini-Meditation

Compassion without power is incomplete.

Meditation

(12 minutes)

1. Imagine a concave area, three to four inches wide, about two inches behind the navel. (The open area faces the navel.)
2. Using the natural voice, intone the syllables "la-oh" fifty times, with the emphasis on the "oh." Hold each "oh" part of the sound for four seconds. Feel the vibration of the sound in the concavity behind the navel.
3. Now make the sound "hoo" ten times, holding each repetition for ten seconds. Feel the vibration of the sound in the throat.
4. Repeat the cycle up to twice more if you wish.
5. The feeling is one of compassion.

Commentary

The sound "la-oh" is beneficial for quickening and opening the heart and the crown simultaneously. The crown is a center above the top of the head that can be pictured as a fountain of effulgent light. The combination of these two sounds helps develop the compassionate nature and tender feelings. In meditation, tenderness and sensitivity are qualities of paramount importance.

In many religions, the sound "hoo" connotes the divine presence. The combination of the "h" sound with the soft vowels evokes nostalgia for states of purity and eternality.

Hint: After doing "la-oh" in a monotone, try doing "la" as a deeper sound and "oh" as a higher sound.

You can find audio demonstrations of meditations in this book, as well as additional resources, at www.UniversalMeditations.com.

Week Ten

Meditations on Sound

Mini-Meditation

The bird in flight has found the secret of transforming earth into heaven.

Meditation

(12 minutes)

1. Using the natural voice, make the sound "hoo" fifteen times. Hold each repetition for ten seconds and feel the vibration in the throat.
2. Now intone the syllable "la" thirty times. Hold each repetition for five seconds; feel the vibration of the sound in the center of the chest.
3. Repeat the cycle up to three times if you wish.
4. The feeling is spiritual or etheric.

Commentary

The combination of "hoo" and "la" acts like an electric current or illuminator of our spirits. If this sound is repeated on a daily basis, you will notice more space developing naturally in your mind, a growing feeling of detachment, and an increase in sensitivity. This practice is also helpful in increasing the creative aspects of our personalities. Try to maintain a feeling of sacredness while intoning these sounds.

You can find audio demonstrations of meditations in this book, as well as additional resources, at www.UniversalMeditations.com.

Week Eleven

Meditations on Sound & Light

INTRODUCTION

This is an expansion of the meditations of Week 10. It is best to do those meditations before doing the ones for this week.

As in Week 10, these meditations require you to make a sound and to use that sound for inner awakening. As before, use your imagination to create the sound inwardly if you are in surroundings where you cannot comfortably voice the sound.

You need not be overly concerned with proper pronunciation. It is more important to listen to whatever sound you produce. It is also important to place the vibration of the sound in the area of the body suggested. It does not matter whether you experience this physically in the body or on a more subtle energetic level. The emphasis must be on the experience itself rather than on any expectation or desire to "do it right."

The same cautions apply as in Week 10. Do not do these exercises while driving. The weekend practice is best done at home, in quiet. If you feel dizzy or lightheaded, stop and breathe a little more deeply. When you begin again, shorten the time you hold each sound.

Remember that the goal of this series is to experience moments of transformative energy, and it may not be necessary to do the full number of repetitions. Pushing to complete the suggested number of repetitions can make it more difficult to focus on sensing the vibration in the body. Try to feel the delicate balance between the sensitivity of the moment and the desire to complete the suggested number of repetitions.

You can find audio demonstrations of meditations in this book, as well as additional resources, at www.UniversalMeditations.com.

MONDAY

Mini-Meditation

Voicing forgiveness to another opens a door.
Feeling forgiveness toward oneself allows
one to walk through it.

Meditation
(6 to 8 minutes)

1. Using your natural voice, intone the syllable "ka" twenty times, holding each repetition for three or four seconds. Try to place the vibration of the sound behind the sternum in the center of the chest. While you are making this sound, envision with the inner eye a bright, butter-yellow light.
2. Switch to the syllable "ga" and repeat the exercise as above. Imagine the light has become more golden, with greater depth and dimensionality.
3. Repeat the above cycle.
4. The feeling is one of forgiveness.

Commentary

The yellow-golden color in this practice is reminiscent of the light of our spirits. There is a reason we value golden metal. We feel a very deep connection with this color in our subconscious, and as we intone this sound, the light will naturally emerge. This color is very healing for the nervous system.

You can find audio demonstrations of meditations in this book, as well as additional resources, at www. UniversalMeditations.com.

Week Eleven

Meditations on Sound & Light

TUESDAY

Mini-Meditation

It is the ego that must surrender,
not the spirit.

Meditation

(10 minutes)

1. Using your natural voice, intone the sound "huiee" forty
   times, holding each repetition for three or four seconds.
   Feel the vibration of the sound in the center of the forehead. While you are making this sound, imagine a very
   soft lilac light, the color and sensation of pre-dawn.
2. Repeat up to two cycles of forty if you wish.
3. The feeling is one of a cool yielding.

Commentary

This lilac color evokes a feeling of loving without emotional baggage. In age, we surrender to the changes of life and accept that life is change itself. This practice promotes a balanced feeling of detachment.

You can find audio demonstrations of meditations in this book, as well as additional resources, at www.UniversalMeditations.com.

WEDNESDAY

Mini-Meditation

If you can lift your own spirits, you can be an aid and a comfort to others.

Meditation

(8 minutes)

1. Imagine a straight line drawn from the top of your head to the back of your tongue, and another drawn through the head from ear to ear. Now imagine a golf-ball-sized space where the two lines intersect.

2. Using your natural voice, make the sound "ong" fifteen times, placing the vibration in the space described above. Hold the sound on "ng" rather than the opening "ah" sound, and hold each repetition for five seconds. While you are making this sound, visualize a peachy-rose-orange that is deep and lit from within.

3. Repeat for up to three cycles of fifteen if you wish.

4. The feeling is one of upliftment.

Commentary

This is a special color for mystics, representing both sunrise and sunset. Some of the great teachers of humanity wore this color, as do the people of some yogic orders and some Buddhist sanghas (communities). Exposure to this color promotes a positive outlook, a caring nature, and strong faith in the balanced personality of God. It is this color that reminds our subconscious that suffering is not eternal, but like the sunrise and sunset, it signals transition. This can be a nice color to include in your home.

You can find audio demonstrations of meditations in this book, as well as additional resources, at www.UniversalMeditations.com.

THURSDAY

Mini-Meditation

That is pure which contains no trace of anything other than itself.

Meditation

(10 to 15 minutes)

1. Using your natural voice, intone the syllable "dom" (rhymes with "mom") fifty times, holding each repetition for two to three seconds. The sound should feel as if it is coming from the lower back. While you are making this sound, imagine a bright, spring-green light, the color of new grass.
2. Now intone the syllable "som" fifty times, again holding each repetition for two to three seconds. The sound should feel as if it is coming from the shoulder blades and the upper back. While you are making this sound, visualize light with the icy blue color of a glacier.
3. Repeat the cycle twice.
4. The feeling is one of purity.

Commentary

Spring green is the color of healing and clear communication. A sore throat can often be helped by wrapping a spring green scarf around your neck and trying to only speak well of people. The icy blue reminds us of a state of consciousness there were no shadows in our minds, no dust particles to re ect the light. Imagining this ice-blue color purifies our bodies, minds, hearts, and souls.

You can find audio demonstrations of meditations in this book, as well as additional resources, at www.UniversalMeditations.com.

FRIDAY

Mini-Meditation

The inner sight is infinite, the outer sight finite. The inner sound is endless, the outer sound limited. The task is to lose the finite in the infinite and emerge again, as the day emerges from the night.

Meditation

(12 minutes)

1. Imagine a concave area, three to four inches wide, about two inches behind the navel. (The open area faces the navel.)
2. Using the natural voice, intone the syllables "la-oh" fifty times, with the emphasis on the "oh." Hold each "oh" part of the sound for three to four seconds. Feel the vibration of the sound in the concavity behind the navel. While you are making this sound, imagine a black light that is crystalline and velvety.
3. Repeat the cycle twice if you wish.
4. The feeling is sel ess and infinite.

Commentary

Some mystics refer to the light of Christ as "the black light."
Another way to think of this is as the light that is so powerful
it swallows up all other light. Many have had the experience
of sensing light in an absolutely dark room. In this practice,
we sense the light in the blackness.

Hint: *Imagine black velvet shimmering with light.*

You can find audio demonstrations of meditations in this book, as well
as additional resources, at www.UniversalMeditations.com.

Week Eleven

Meditations on Sound & Light

WEEKEND

Mini-Meditation

The nomad wisely travels at night unless he or she must travel by day.

Meditation

(12 minutes)

1. Using the natural voice, make the sound "hoo" fifteen times. Hold each repetition for ten seconds and feel the vibration in the throat. While you are making this sound, imagine a clear, shimmering light, like the light rising off of desert sand.
2. Repeat the cycle up to three times if you wish.
3. The feeling is one of mildness and refinement yet infinitely powerful.

Commentary

Clear light is the color of ecstasy. As our consciousness changes from interacting solely with the material world, to experiencing the world that is transcendent, our relationship with light changes. As our breath becomes more refined, we perceive objects not just by the light that is re ected from them, but by the light they generate as well. Today there is much fascination with the aura. Behind the aura is the clear light of oneness.

You can find audio demonstrations of meditations in this book, as well as additional resources, at www.UniversalMeditations.com.

Week Twelve

Meditations on the Self

INTRODUCTION

This challenging series of meditations combines a gentle movement of the body with real exploration of the self. So many moments of our lives are spent objectifying others that we lack the sensitivity to experience ourselves beyond divisive and critical thinking.

In this series of meditations, we are asked to experience our nature and personality as gifts from a loving universe. Even though we might notice our limitations and faults, the rhythmic continuity of these meditations enables us to experience ourselves beyond our limited nature.

MEDITATIONS ON THE SELF

MONDAY

Mini-Meditation

Forgiveness is the signature of a mature human being and of healthy relationships.

Meditation
(7 to 10 minutes)

1. Gently dropping your head, speak softly into your heart, "I forgive you." Slowly raising your head, say, "You forgive me." Continuing the head motions, repeat "I forgive you," "You forgive me" eleven times.

2. As above, speak softly into your heart, "I forgive" and silently think the word "you." Raising the head, say, "You forgive" and silently think the word "me." Continuing the head motions, repeat "I forgive [you]," "You forgive [me]" eleven times.

3. As above, silently think the word "I," speak softly into your heart "forgive," and silently think the word "you." Raising the head, silently think the word "you," say "forgive" aloud, and silently think the word "me." Continuing the

head motions, repeat "[I] forgive [you]," [You] forgive [me]" eleven times.

4. Continuing the head motions, think silently on the out-breath into the heart, "I forgive you." Raising the head on the in-breath, think "You forgive me." Silently repeat on the breath, "I forgive you," "You forgive me" eleven times.

5. Sit in silence for one minute.

Commentary

For many people, there is a certain charge around the word forgiveness. Some feel they are not able to forgive; some feel they give up their power by forgiving; some feel they are being manipulated by guilt and will be much happier if they don't forgive; and some feel the very act is artificial. Forgiveness is an energy that is ever-present. All we have to do is turn and face it. By being aware of forgiveness in relation to a person or a situation, the forgiveness will do the forgiving, not our egos.

This meditation helps us experience the inner truth that there is no benefit in withholding forgiveness. It guides us gently into the stream of forgiveness without the concepts of "should" and "good," which often just create guilt. A lack of the experience of forgiveness will inhibit the evolution of those who are seriously committed to a spiritual path.

Tuesday

Mini-Meditation

Humanity, by forgetting adoration, has clothed itself in the darkness of separation.

Meditation

(7 to 10 minutes)

1. Gently dropping your head, speak softly into your heart, "I adore you." Slowly raising your head, say, "You adore me." Continuing the head motions, repeat "I adore you," "You adore me" eleven times.

2. As above, speak softly into your heart, "I adore" and silently think the word "you." Raising the head, say, "You adore" and silently think the word "me." Continuing the head motions, repeat "I adore [you]," "You adore [me]" eleven times.

3. As above, silently think the word "I," speak softly into your heart "adore," and silently think the word "you." Raising the head, silently think the word "you," say "adore" aloud, and silently think the word "me." Continuing the head motions, repeat "[I] adore [you]," "[You] adore [me]" eleven times.

4. Continuing the head motions, think silently on the out-breath into the heart, "I adore you." On the in-breath, think "You adore me." Silently repeat on the breath, "I adore you," "You adore me" eleven times.
5. Sit in silence for one minute.

Commentary

This is one of those meditations that we believe will be so awkward and that makes us so self-conscious we are almost embarrassed to try it. We have little resistance to the adoration of God, the prophets, people we idealize, even material things. In this meditation, we are training ourselves not to adore our false ego, but to adore the miracle of our own creation and existence. Each human being is unique and worthy of the emotion we usually reserve for our deepest beloveds. As we learn to relate to our self in a loving and glorious way, this loving relationship expands to those around us and ultimately to the way we relate to all people. This practice is on the path of the royal yoga, uniting the limited with the limitless. It recognizes, and enables us to awaken, the divinity in each human being.

WEDNESDAY

Mini-Meditation

Understanding the mystery of breath is a worthwhile goal for any lifetime.

Meditation

(7 to 10 minutes)

1. Gently dropping your head, speak softly into your heart, "I breathe you." Slowly raising your head, say, "You breathe me." Continuing the head motions, repeat "I breathe you," "You breathe me" eleven times.

2. As above, speak softly into your heart, "I breathe" and silently think the word "you." Raising the head, say, "You breathe" and silently think the word "me." Continuing the head motions, repeat "I breathe [you]," "You breathe [me]" eleven times.

3. As above, silently think the word "I," speak softly into your heart "breathe," and silently think the word "you." Raising the head, silently think the word "you," say "breathe" aloud, and silently think the word "me." Con-

tinuing the head motions, repeat "[I] breathe [you]," "[You] breathe [me]" eleven times.

4. Continuing the head motions, think silently on the out-breath, "I breathe you." On the in-breath, think "You breathe me." Silently repeat on the breath, "I breathe you," "You breathe me" eleven times.

5. Sit in silence for one minute.

Commentary

There is a wonderful analogy made about the relationship of human beings and God. A fish is always swimming in water. The water is coming into the fish, giving it life, becoming part of the fish, and leaving the fish. Yet the fish does not have the ability to know that water exists until it is taken out of water. We are not just talking about air in this meditation. Here, when I say "breathe," I am referring to the all-pervading consciousness moving through us, as we move through it.

THURSDAY

Mini-Meditation

There are no walls in spirit, only doors.

Meditation

(7 to 10 minutes)

1. Gently dropping your head, speak softly into your heart, "I spirit you." Slowly raising your head, say, "You spirit me." Continuing the head motions, repeat "I spirit you," "You spirit me" eleven times.

2. As above, speak softly into your heart, "I spirit" and silently think the word "you." Raising the head, say, "You spirit" and silently think the word "me." Continuing the head motions, repeat "I spirit [you]," "You spirit [me]" eleven times.

3. As above, silently think the word "I," speak softly into your heart "spirit," and silently think the word "you." Raising the head, silently think the word "You," say "spirit" aloud, and silently think the word "me." Continuing the head motions, repeat "[I] spirit [you]," "[You] spirit [me]" eleven times.

4. Continuing the head motions, think silently on the out-breath, "I spirit you." On the in-breath, think, "You spirit me." Silently repeat on the breath, "I spirit you," "You spirit me" eleven times.
5. Sit in silence for one minute.

Commentary

The sense of spirit is clearer when it is used both as a noun and a verb. Spirit is active, connective, creative, and all-encompassing. A specific mood arises naturally from this meditation. Try not to create a mood, a feeling, or an experience. The very word spirit brings with it many levels of experience. There is a saying: Heart speaks to heart, spirit to spirit. When Jewish families celebrate the Passover Seder, at one point the youngest child opens the front door of the home and invites in the spirit of the Prophet Elijah. The innocence in the child creates a home for the spirit of the prophet. Bring that innocence to this meditation.

FRIDAY

Mini-Meditation

One of our great faults as human beings is to limit love to that which we can understand. By doing so, we place our understanding above love.

Meditation
(7 to 10 minutes)

1. Gently dropping your head, speak softly into your heart, "I love you." Slowly raising your head, say, "You love me." Continuing the head motions, repeat "I love you," "You love me" eleven times.

2. As above, speak softly into your heart, "I love" and silently think the word "you." Raising the head, say, "You love" and silently think the word "me." Continuing the head motions, repeat "I love [you]," "You love [me]" eleven times.

3. As above, silently think the word "I," speak softly into your heart "love," and silently think the word "you." Raising the head, silently think the word "You," say "love"

aloud, and silently think the word "me." Continuing the head motions, repeat "[I] love [you]," "[You] love [me]" eleven times.

4. Continuing the head motions, think silently on the out-breath, "I love you." On the in-breath, think "You love me." Silently repeat on the breath, "I love you," "You love me" eleven times.

5. Sit in silence for one minute.

Commentary

These words, "I love you," may have more meanings projected onto them than any other words. This meditation can help to quell those projections and allow us to actually feel the words. Love is incredibly resilient. As soon as you remove the projections, love's true nature shines forth resplendently. To know love is to know God. To know love is to know the very essence of the human being. Even the sound of this word has an effect on the human heart. Try this meditation without placing any burden or expectation on the word "love." Be a visitor from another planet who hasn't been conditioned to respond in any way to this word. Let it come and feel what happens.

WEEKEND

Mini-Meditation

What we call feeling is really the waves on the surface of the sea. In the depth of the sea, true feeling waits.

Meditation

(20 to 40 minutes)

1. Find a quiet space where you can spend twenty to forty minutes uninterrupted. Repeat this week's cycle of meditations, beginning as follows:

2. Gently dropping your head, speak softly into your heart, "I forgive you." Slowly raising your head, say, "You forgive me." Continuing the head motions, repeat "I forgive you," "You forgive me" eleven times.

3. As above, speak softly into your heart, "I forgive" and silently think the word "you." Raising the head, say, "You forgive" and silently think the word "me." Continuing the head motions, repeat "I forgive [you]," "You forgive [me]" eleven times.

4. As above, silently think the word "I," speak softly into

your heart "forgive," and silently think the word "you." Raising the head, silently think the word "You," say "forgive" aloud, and silently think the word "me." Continuing the head motions, repeat "[I] forgive [you]," "[You] forgive [me]" eleven times.

5. Continuing the head motions, think silently on the outbreath, "I forgive you." On the in-breath, think, "You forgive me." Silently repeat on the breath, "I forgive you," "You forgive me" eleven times.

6. Sit in silence for one minute.

7. Now repeat the cycle, using the words "adore," "breathe," "spirit," and "love." Pause after each cycle to quietly take notice of your feeling state.

Commentary

It can be very helpful when practicing a long meditation with different attributes to keep paper and pen by your side. As you have different feelings or experiences, jot down a note or two as reminders. After the meditation, you might want to write a longer description of each section. Reading the descriptions later can almost immediately bring you back into the meditative state.

CLOSING CIRCLE

I offer this book as a gift from the many wonderful and profound human beings who have made the inner world a real and valuable part of their lives. Their prayers and meditations over the last eons, we hope, will be inherited by us, enhanced and passed on to the next generation. In this way, the path to peace and inner joy will continually evolve, and the gift of our ancestors will grow.

BLESSINGS

The blessings of nature, the blessings of children, the blessings of innocence, the blessings of the earth, the blessings of the water, the blessings of the fire and the air are available to all who open their hearts and minds. Emerging out of all of these blessings is the nectar of kindness which enlightens and sweetens us.

It is my hope that this book will enable you to experience all the most wonderful gifts and blessings that the universe can provide for us in this life.

May all beings be well, May all beings be happy,

Peace. Peace. Peace.